Tactical Survival

Steven Varnell

The author is not engaged in rendering legal advice or services to the individual reader. The ideas, procedures, and suggestions contained in this book are not intended as a substitute for following all applicable laws in any reader's jurisdiction. Neither the author nor the publisher shall be responsible for any loss or damage allegedly arising from any information or suggestion in this book. The author and publisher disclaim any responsibility for any adverse effects or consequences from the misapplication or injudicious use of the information presented in this text. Anyone practicing the skills presented in this book should do so only after permission of a licensed medical profession. You may be or cause injury to another if you train or apply the techniques used in this book. Neither the author nor the publisher is responsible for any such injury that may result.

While the author has made every effort to provide accurate information at the time of publication, neither the author nor the publisher assumes any responsibility for errors, or for changes that occur after publication. Further, neither the author nor the publisher assumes any responsibility for third party websites or their content.

Also by Steven Varnell

Criminal Interdiction

I dedicate this book to all of the officers who are standing the wall.

CONTENTS

ACKNOWLEDGMENTS

I have to, without doubt, give thanks to my wonderful and patient wife. She has learned this patience from the years I was on the job and now with my passion to continue to learn and teach. For my son who is among the many standing the wall and daughter who also has found her passion in teaching.

To the many officers that had to listen, and always without complaint, my ideas for this book and for providing their insights. All of the information and ideas contained herein are my own, but was collected off the backs of those who walked the walk before and after me. May God Bless you all.

INTRODUCTION

This book was started as I hear the news about another police officer being gunned down in America. Sadly, it is now two. At the same time, I listen to what I consider "idiots" complaining about police brutality at the "occupy protest." Fortunately, they are the minority of the population. Some people will disagree with anything from the government regardless who's in charge, Republican or Democrat. There is this small disillusioned subculture that has lost all sense of reasonableness. To this minority, there is no faction of the government which can function properly unless it is to hand out free money. Never mind the simple fact that the majority of our problems are a result of our own doing.

Personal responsibility and common sense are the keys to solving most of our issues. The old adage of, "if it is too good to be true, then it probably is," would have prevented most financial problems. Stay on a true and tried course instead of a get rich quick scam. Everything turns out for the best when common sense and hard work are applied together to accomplish goals. On the other hand, we all know there are many among us who do not want to put forth the efforts. They do not want the true and tried course. They cheat the system and others to do the work for them. This apathy often guides them into a life of crime, violence, and an eventual confrontation with the police. It is at this juncture that we must be prepared to survive the encounter.

I have developed an idea or mantra that I like to use; **Study Train Survive**. It is my way to remember and teach others about taking a multifaceted approach to resolve our problems. In most jobs the philosophy is the same. You are hired and required to become familiar with the companies inner workings before receiving the initial training for a specific job. The training will continue if it is a good and progressive company. Survival means to study and train hard. Otherwise, someone more dedicated comes along and your seeking another job.

For law enforcement, the basic premise is the same. Once hired, the studies initiate at the Academy followed by a training process. I refer to this as a training process and not a program because at some point, a program finishes. A process is a continuing learning endeavor which has no end. Training is nonstop as you are constantly striving to improve your skills. The difference lies in the end result. Death and injury are the consequences for failing to partake in the task of **Study Train Survive** as a law enforcement officer.

The general public walks around each day without observing any situational awareness. They are future victims. There are many predators on earth, and too many among the general populace are idealist without reasonable and realistic views of the world. They are the wandering sheep grazing on the beautiful green pastures, never cognizant of the fact that they are watched nearly every day by a wolf. Law enforcement does it best to protect us, and they do a good job. However, most police officers spend their days responding to the events that have already occurred.

Be proactive by not waiting for someone else for protection. How many times have you heard somebody say, "I cannot believe this has happened to me?" Generally, had people maintained some situational awareness, whatever occurred may have never happened. I will repeat it after every section because I want you to remember, **Study Train Survive**.

Use this book as a guide. It will cover the various topics having the greatest impact to the welfare of law enforcement. These are the essential areas where an officer may be injured in an encounter with an asshole. I want anyone who reads this to know that though I write from the perspective of a police officer, it also applies to civilian encounters. You do not have to be in law enforcement to follow these lessons because they are all about personal safety.

In *Criminal Interdiction,* I explained our primary responsibility as: "Have you ever thought about the reason why there really are police officers? There are many academics who can give you the text book versions why, but for me it is just two words; Asshole Confrontation." A year later, I still cannot find a better explanation for what we do. The problem is that so many officers continue to be injured and killed. By the end of the year 2011, the number of police officers killed in the line of duty by gunfire increased by 15% over the previous year and remains the number one cause of death. In Los Angeles, the number of incidents where officers have been shot at has increased by 29%. Crime will continue to maintain these levels and may increase. One can only surmise that so will the violence.

The current state of the economy will assist in dictating desperate people's actions. Everyone, civilians and officers alike, must be on a heightened sense of self- protection. I wish more people would read this book, *Criminal Interdiction,* and other titles dedicated to saving lives. For those who have studied these, you're thinking. It is the beginning phase of my adage, **Study Train Survive**. If only a single bit of information is retained, it may make a difference. Always thinking and concentrating at the task at hand is a game changer. We already know how difficult it is to maintain this constant vigilance. I want you to remember the lessons learned, add to them if needed, change some if necessary, and adjust it to the job while insisting your partners do the same.

When working interdiction three things must occur: the identification of the criminal, the seizure of the criminal and evidence, and a successful prosecution. If any of these factors are missing, the *Criminal Interdiction* was not successful. If the criminal is not recognized, the evidence and prosecution never takes place. If the criminal is identified, but the evidence is not found, there is no prosecution. If the criminal is identified and the evidence found, but the prosecution is not accomplished, then the interdiction was a failure. Sure the contraband was taken from the streets, however, the criminal was also returned to cause more harm. Do your job with diligence, safety, and completely within the laws of your jurisdiction. When this is performed, you are providing absolute protection to your community.

This book is broken down into various topics by chapters. The situations are wide-ranging and are my opinion, based on nearly 30 years of law enforcement. It is alright to disagree with the ideas. As I have explained before, the goal is to get you to think. Read about the techniques that I have used successfully and tweak them for yourself. The basis for them all are solid, however, no two people are alike and prefer things done in a certain manner. My only warning is not to be so closed minded as to not at least try these techniques, because they can save your life. I know they have saved mine. Go out and seek the assholes while being fully prepared to deal with them. For those of you not in law enforcement, I say learn to recognize them for your own protection. They are around all of the time. Watching and waiting for that opportunity to cause physical or emotional damages. Together we can make a difference. The wolves are stalking. The sheepdogs are watching. The sheep are always grazing with their heads in the grass.

Study Train Survive

1 TRAFFIC STOPS

It's amazing to me how we lose sight of the big picture with a single
focus.

Traffic stops are the one activity that law enforcement conducts
each day more than any other. To coincide with this volume of
contact, they are also one of the most dangerous and important
crime-fighting tool in our arsenal. Every criminal before, during, or
after every offense enters a motor vehicle. Our society is very
mobile. This mobility affords criminals the opportunities to carry out
and/or flee their crimes. Therefore, I will cover this event first.

In 2011, there were 26 police officers murdered by gunfire
during a traffic event. Of these, four were by ambush while sitting in
their car, and three occurred while the officers were not engaged in a
specific law enforcement activity other than patrol. Additionally,
nine officers were killed when they conducted pedestrian stops. In
addition to these poor souls, another 59 police officers have been
killed in 2011 as a result of some type of vehicle accident. Though
gunfire has overtaken auto accidents as the primary cause of death,
when you combine the vehicle accident aspect with the gunfire
deaths during some type of traffic stop, the total becomes 85.

According to the Officer Down Memorial Page (ODMP), the total number of officers killed in the line of duty during 2011 totals 166. Therefore, over 50% of all officers deaths are related to vehicles and traffic stops. It is the single most dangerous thing we do.

Traffic stops are considered routine by many in law enforcement. We conduct them each day without any serious occurrence. According to the Bureau of Justice Statistics, only 1.6% of all traffic stops result in the occupants of the cars having force used against them. Each year there are over 43 million traffic stops conducted and only 5% are searched.

How often does your agency study and train for traffic stops? Because of the volume of work involved, we should train each year the safety aspects of a stop. Even though I spent years training other officers and worked the street right up to the day I retired, I never stopped training. Appendix I, at the end of this book is a list of training courses I received during my career. You can see which areas of law enforcement fascinated me as I perceived each of these classes as a new experience. It was like seeing practical aspects of topics through other people's eyes.

Conducting a traffic stop involves a series or checklist of things to accomplish. It all begins with the identification of the vehicle you want to stop. Most officer's race up to the targeted car with their emergency equipment activated. I am telling everyone now, slow down and approach with ease. Take these moments of approach and watch the behaviors of the occupants in the car. Watch everyone to see if they appear calm or nervous. Is the driver overly watching you in their rear and side view mirrors? Are the passengers behaving the same as they were when you first saw them? Notice the windows of the vehicle as they pass and again after you have caught up to the car. If they were up or partially down and now completely down, assume they are trying to air out the car.

Watch for bumper stickers, air fresheners, rental car information, bibles on the dash or other religious gear. In and of themselves, they may not be important, but when applied with other items, they may be the beginning of a *Criminal Interdiction*. Take the time to study common items of paraphernalia, including gang signs of significance. Be cognizant of as much as possible and this extra effort will help you survive and make good arrest. Be aware of the gangs that are in the areas of your patrol. Their building tags, colors, and other articles can influence the stop. Gang and certain types of religious symbolism's can have specific meanings of their intentions. Photos, statues, medallions, or tattoos of Jesus Malverde or Santa Muerte can indicate they are transporting contraband or have a connection with the business.

Jesus Malverde   Santa Muerte

How long did it take for the vehicle to stop after you activated your emergency equipment? Again watch the behaviors of the vehicle occupants for changes now that they know they are being stopped. All of the vehicle's information should have already been radioed in or ran on your computer. Standing roadside with the violator is not the time to discover that the car is stolen or the subject of a Be On the Look Out (BOLO). Move the stop if the targeted vehicle stop's in an unsafe location.

Remove your seat belt before coming to a complete stop to prevent being tangled when exiting. Watch their brake lights and turn signals. If they left one or both on, use it as a warning that the driver of the car is nervous and is too focused on you. It is a form of audio occlusion.

Stop your vehicle as far as possible from the traveled portion of the road. The distance between your vehicle and the violators should be at least two car lengths. This provides you with some response time should the occupants take any offensive actions after the stop. If you park too close, they can be at the front of your car before you can react; an easy shot for most people. Distance is always our friend.

After the stop you start the approach. Be sure everyone stays inside of the car. If someone exits without permission, order them back. Failure to comply with this order should definitely place you on alert. Maintain distance and observe while calling for assistance. Never be on equal grounds with anyone. Deploy whatever tools are necessary for the situation.

If possible, approach the car on the passengers' side. Not only is it a better tactical position from the vehicles occupants, it will also provide you some protection from approaching traffic. Remember that your vehicle is parked about two car lengths back. If it is struck by another vehicle, it will absorb a lot of the energy from the impact. Additionally, you have the added protection of their car to deflect additional forces before being struck as a pedestrian.

From the passengers' side of their car, you can see most of the interior. When they open the glove box, the entire compartment is visible. Most people are right handed. Those who are left handed and intended to pull a gun, will hide it in their right hand because they expect you to walk to their drivers window. If you stop behind the "B" pillar or front door window frame, the driver would have to raise the gun above the seat, and back to shoot at you. A few steps rearward and they will not have a shot, but you will. If there is a front seat passenger, the driver will have to sweep the gun over them to shoot. The passengers side is unequivocally the best place to stand during a traffic stop because you have advantages over the occupants and approaching traffic. Several officers have been shot while on the passengers side of the car. No position is perfect, however, the videos shows the officers are literally standing in the passengers window. They walk right up to the window and bend down to see inside. Start observing everyone as you walk up to the car, again nearing their rear side windows, and STOP before reaching the front passengers window. If the windows are tinted, have the occupants roll them all down before making the approach.

If you are pulling over a tractor trailer, do not stop behind the vehicle. Drive to the front where you are in a position to watch the driver and see if there are any passengers. This can be done along the shoulder to a position forward and beside the tractor or passing and stopping at the same position in the front. The driver can be observed if they attempt to hide or do anything which could harm you.

The standard practice of positioning your patrol car behind a tractor trailer does not have any tactical advantages. If any oncoming traffic leaves the road you could be crushed against the trailer. How often do you see officers exit and stand around waiting for the driver to walk back? Often they will have to cover almost 60 feet to reach you. If they walk down the traffic side of the truck, they risk being struck by passing traffic. Once they clear the back of the trailer, they are instantly in front of you. If they intend you harm, there is little time or space to prepare for it. In order to watch the driver walk back, you have to stand close to the passing traffic. Just drive along the side of the truck after it has stopped. Position your car at an angle to the side and front of the tractor. Now everything can be seen inside the cab.

I have had several officers question this tactic. When they are standing around at the back of a truck, with no idea who is inside or what they are doing, and then waiting for them to walk back, you may change your mind. Every officer who has tried this tactic has adjusted the way they stop trucks. Once used, you will see exactly how effective and tactically sound it is compared to just standing at the back of a trailer. For a more detailed description of all of the above actions please refer to chapter 5 and 13 in *Criminal Interdiction,* which are entire chapters dedicated to these actions.

Study Train Survive

Summary of Traffic Stops:

- Identify the vehicle you want to stop. Do not race up to the car with your emergency equipment activated. Ease up to the them to observe their behaviors.

- Begin taking a mental inventory of the things you see, e.g., bumper stickers, air fresheners, or rentals.

- Observe the actions of the driver when they pull off the road. Did they travel some distance or stop immediately?

- Be sure the area of the stop is safe when outside of your vehicle.

- Position your vehicle completely off the road, if possible.

- Be sure you are already prepared to exit your vehicle at the time of the stop.

- Stop your vehicle about two cars lengths back. Remember, distance is for your benefit.

- Make sure everyone stays in the car.

- Watch for the brake lights and turn signals. Are they still own?

- If possible, always approach on the passengers side.

- When stopping tractor trailers, do not stop behind them as with cars. Drive to the front of the vehicle where you can observe the drivers actions.

- **Study Train Survive**

2 PEDESTRIAN ENCOUNTERS

"When things go wrong, simplify."

Olympic weightlifting coach Dan John – Never Let Go: A philosophy of Lifting

(This makes so much sense to me. Simplify has always been my theory to solve problems. When things go wrong, most people complicate the theory.)

It was mentioned in the last chapter that nine police officers have been killed in the line of duty by gunfire from pedestrian encounters. This equates to one officer killed by a pedestrian every 1.7 months.

Similar to vehicle stops, pedestrian stops can have additional dangers. When stopping a vehicle, we know that we want the occupants to remain inside of the car. They are on equal footing when outside. You must always maintain a position of advantage. With the pedestrian, they are already outside and have the initial position of advantage. They can approach before you have the opportunity to exit your vehicle. Therefore, you must try to come up from behind and stop your car prior to passing. Your car should be parked at least two car lengths from the subject. This gives you time to exit before they can respond or provides the distance needed to react to any actions they take.

Sometimes it will help if you see the pedestrian that you want to encounter and drive past them. However, this tactic does remove the element of surprise. After driving past them, they may expose feelings of guilt upon seeing a police officer. Their behaviors may change or they could take evasive actions. Either way, this will tell you that the person is not your average citizen. Generally, people are not surprised or nervous by the sight of a police officer, unless they have done something wrong. Any person deserves your attention when there is a change in their behavior.

Do not immediately turn back around if you just drove past the subject. Drive a short distance and watch their conduct in your rear view mirrors. Observe and take note of any and all clothing, including hats, shirt, pants, shoes, jackets, and colors. Guess the subjects physical dimensions and watch for facial hair, tattoos, etc. The more information wrote down before the encounter the less you will have to take your eyes off the subject during the stop. Furthermore, should the suspect flee on foot or commit an assault, you will have a detailed description to report to responding officers. How often has someone fled and all we can give is a sketchy description at best? This is the time for you to observe their attire in relation to the weather. Is the person wearing a jacket on a warm day? Maybe they are wearing a heavy jacket on a cool day. Are their pants baggie? Can you see any bulges in their clothing? Are they wearing several pairs of pants? If so, this means they will have several layers of pockets, which will have to be searched, if you arrest them.

Do they have a standard gait or is it exaggerated? Watch their hand and arm movements. When people are carrying illegal items under their attire they have a tendency to touch them. A subject carrying a gun in their waistband will frequently brush against it with their arm or hand,which will show in the way they walk. The bad guys needs assurance that their weapon stays in place, especially when they see the police. Police officers have a tendency to not move their strong side arm as much as their weak. Sometimes, there will be more of an arc to their strong side arm. This allows the hand and arm to pass around your holstered weapon, which stands out from the side of your body. We get so used to this walk that when out of uniform, our strong arm arcs around the hip.

An example of this behavior was conducted by a television show. They placed a sign on the sidewalk in Las Vegas that read, "Check your wallet." Nearly everyone who walked by the sign reached down with their hand and touched their billfold. What this actually provided was the exact location of their wallet. "Reformed" pick pocket artist were standing around the area and watching where they touched. They could then use this information to steal from that exact spot on the person.

If you know you will be stopping this subject, be sure to take off the seat belt, turn on the hand held radio, and notify dispatch of your location. Therefore, the moment you stop, immediately exit the car with your full attention on the pedestrian. You can call out to the subject, but maintain distance. Be sure their hands are out of their pockets and remain in sight. Keep in mind it is the hands which will hurt you by striking, drawing a knife, a gun, or other weapon. Knowing exactly where their hands are the entire time is paramount to your safety.

Never drive up to any person on the streets, whether a pedestrian, a disabled vehicle, or any other type of event, and stay in your car. You never want to place yourself in such a position of disadvantage. As an example of the dangers involved with this action, this is a quote taken from a New Jersey newspaper article at nbcnewyork.com:

"She said the officer was conducting "a routine stop" of the subject, chatting with him in a non-confrontational way for a few minutes, leading authorities to believe the two may have been acquainted with each other before the shooting. She said. "The individual stepped back and suddenly pulled out a handgun and shot the officer."

While talking to this pedestrian, the officer never got out of his patrol car, nor had an opportunity to draw his weapon. Unfortunately, this encounter resulted in the officer being shot in the head and killed. Never turn your back to a suspect, and always maintain a visual on them. Stay just out of arms reach, the further the better. As we have learned before, try to have another unit present if you intend to do a pat down. Keep the following informational statistics from the FBI in mind as we confront suspects.

1. 38% of all officers killed in the United States occurred during a crime in progress.

2. 60% of those officers were killed while attempting to make an arrest before their backup had arrived.

3. 68% of those officers died at night.

4. In a physical confrontation with a suspect, 86% of those officers ended up on the ground. 25% of those officers were seriously injured and 12% of that group was killed with their own weapon or secondary weapon.

Study Train Survive

Summary of Pedestrian Encounters:

- Pedestrian stops are similar to vehicle stops except the pedestrians position on foot gives them a temporary advantage.

- If possible, make an initial pass of the subject to observe their behaviors towards you. Your awareness should heighten if there are any behavioral changes.

- Try to write down or call in as much descriptive information about the subject before the encounter.

- Watch for bulges or the customary arm/hand touching of any item they are carrying.

- Approach from behind and have everything ready the moment your car stops so you can exit unimpeded.

- Even if you know the individuals, never sit in your car and talk to them. Under no circumstances should an officer sit in their car after approaching any person. This is a complete lack of situational awareness, for anyone could walk up to you from any direction. This includes disabled vehicles.

- Never turn your back on the subject(s).

- Always watch their hands and make sure they keep them where you can see them.

- If possible, never try to pat down a suspect until back up arrives.

- **Study Train Survive**

3 **FOOT PURSUITS**

"Strong in emotion, weak in tactics"

From a Federal lawsuit against the Philadelphia Police Department in regards to police shootings after a foot pursuit.

There were five police officers shot and killed while engaged in foot pursuits in 2011. Countless others were injured while in pursuits or by the suspects they were chasing. Most agencies have no policies at all, nor do they train their officers in the tactics of foot pursuits. Many never contemplate the inherent dangers associated with pursuits because they become overwhelmed with the adrenaline rush and the desire to arrest the bad guy. There are certain risk indicators that suggest it is important for law enforcement to manage these events. Faced with increasing pursuits and officer injuries, some agencies have sought outside assistance in understanding these dangers. One such study was conducted for the Los Angeles County Sheriffs Office in 2010.

The University of South Carolina initiated the study entitled "A Descriptive Analysis of Foot Pursuits in the Los Angeles County Sheriff's Department." Information was collected on 100 foot pursuits. The researchers found that suspects threatened pursuing deputies with the use of a firearm or other weapon 15 times, or 5.7% of the incidents. Suspects assaulted the deputies in 42% of the occurrences and were armed 23% of the time. 73% of those pursued had a prior criminal arrest record. Because of enhanced prison time for repeat offenders, increased hazards to the officers exist due to the suspect's motivation to resist. Suspects were impaired with drugs, alcohol, or mental illness in 41% of the pursuits. Use of force incidents are much higher than normal with 38% involving hand to hand tactics and 25% involving the use of impact weapons. 60% resulted in force-related injuries to the suspects and 17% of the deputies were injured.

There are definitive tactics for a foot pursuit. First we must all overcome the appeal of an instant arrest. It is not a personal vendetta against you when a subject runs away from a traffic stop or other encounter. If you are alone during an encounter and a subject sprints from the scene, does it make any sense to chase them while leaving your patrol car unattended? I have been in several scenarios of the officer returning from a foot chase to discover his patrol car has been stolen or burglarized.

There is not as much respect for law enforcement as in the past. In some areas, what greater neighborhood reverence would befall upon one who would steal a police car? Then there is the decision of whether this person has committed a crime that warrants a pursuit or do you have proper identification to file charges? Additionally, if there are more subjects at the scene when one ran away, they cannot be expected to still be there when you return.

There are decisions which need to be considered before initiating a pursuit. Are you fit enough to conduct the chase? Is there available backup? Can you dispatch your exact location, suspect description, and direction of travel? What type of area are you in? If it is a crowded neighborhood or housing project, can you maintain a safe pursuit? Do you have a decisive plan of action once the suspect is caught?

Once you have decided to initiate the chase, try to keep your pace to a jog. The suspect will be sprinting and will soon run out of energy. Even if you are in great shape, the 20 plus pounds of extra equipment will exhaust you. Try to keep the suspect in sight and observe his behaviors. Watch his hands in case he reaches into his clothing for a weapon or contraband. Be cognizant of the available cover which is around in the event the suspect turns with a weapon. Watch the actions of the suspect as they run around corners. Does it appear they are trying to maintain their speed or are they trying to slow down? This can indicate their intentions of ambush. Once they are out of sight, you are no longer in control of this situation. Do not let adrenaline cause you to run blindly around the same corner. Many officers have been killed or injured at corners around the country. Jogging keeps that over-reaction of your ego in check and allows for a clear thinking mind. Mental preparedness is half the fight.

You approach the corner where you lost sight of the suspect. It did not appear they slowed down. This is not self-evidence that the offender continued to run. You can try to "cut the pie" by keeping distance from the corner and slowly rounding the apex to view the other side in "slices." This action will equalize the situation if the suspect has set up an ambush. If you went past the corner, the advantage is 100% with the offender. By "cutting the pie" you will probably see each other at the same time. If there are cars and/or trees opposite the corner, a different option would be to swing wide and maintain cover behind those objects while observing the target area.

Another tactic is to stop at the corner, several feet from the wall. Do a quick peek with one eye around the corner. It has to be fast and expose only the portion of your face to see around the edge. If they are waiting in ambush, they will try to shoot at center mass. A simple peek will not afford them the opportunity for the trap. The downside to this method is taking in enough information during the quick peek to feel confident that the suspect is not waiting for you.

Keep your gun holstered during these pursuits. If you catch them or if they surrender, then draw your weapon. Think about being exhausted at the end of the chase and the suspect fights back. Your firearm can be taken away. Recently in California, a Riverside police officer was involved in a foot pursuit. During the chase, the officer was holding his service weapon when he tripped, fell, and the gun was knocked out of his grasp. The suspect saw this happen and ran back to the officer. He struck the officer multiple times with a pipe before grabbing the firearm and killing him.

What is your plan of action once you have caught the offender? There are issues to consider before faced with this situation. Will you maintain distance and hold them at gunpoint or a taser? Will you attempt to handcuff them? Do backup units know your exact location and do you know theirs? Remember, the above study showed that the officers were assaulted in 42% of the cases and use of force is much higher in these adrenaline charged incidents. Mentally prepare with a response appropriate decision. If you know they are unarmed, deploy a secondary weapon. Always maintain a distinct advantage. Should they respond with any type of weapon, decide if the advantage is still yours with the weapon deployed or transition to your firearm. Planning will assist in a quick decision.

Often during a chase, the suspect jumps a fence. If it is a privacy fence and the subject cannot be seen, do not jump at the same location. Again, this is a perfect ambush location. They will expect you to cross where they choose. Move down and find a place to see the other side and then climb over, if it is clear.

The first unit that arrives should be your backup unit. Direct the other units to initiate a tight perimeter to cause the offender to go into hiding. Containment is the best-case scenario for K9 and air services to quickly find them.

K9 will need the exact location where you last saw the suspect and their direction of travel. They will need the type of crime the subject is accused of and any information on weapons. In most jurisdictions, there are specific guidelines for the deployment of K9 and whether the handler can release the dog to bite.

Have another officer go to the original scene from where the offender initially ran. If there is a vehicle or other information available, try to obtain identification and affiliation with the area that may provide intelligence as to where they are running. We are all creatures of habit and most people will try to go somewhere familiar. Have several units go to this location to see if the suspect is there or if anyone may know of their whereabouts.

Study Train Survive

Summary of Foot Pursuits:

- Foot pursuits should not be conducted alone.

- Very good radio communication is essential for both you and the responding units.

- If alone, initiate if you can keep the suspect in sight. Maintain surveillance of the subject while relaying accurate information to assisting units.

- Follow sound situational awareness ideas for areas which provide you cover.

- Never pursue a subject into a building or any area where you cannot maintain good visuals and have sufficient cover.

- Most subjects will try and hide once they have lost the initial officer. Be a great witness with a good physical description and wait for backup, K9, and air services.

- Try jogging instead of sprinting. Remember that we are wearing extra weight with our equipment. Let the suspect exhaust themselves with sprinting. Otherwise, you may not have the energy reserves to protect yourself. Know your own physical limitations.

- If the suspect goes around the edge of a building, this is a classic ambush point. NEVER run around that same corner. People anticipate you to follow the same path. Move out wide and slow down. This wide angle can give you a greater advantage. Cut the pie, try a quick peek, or swing out wide with available cover.

- Solid tactics and commitment to training can save lives.

- **Study Train Survive**

4 HANDS ON

"Simplicity is a powerful principle that allows us to channel our energy like a laser beam and avoid getting stuck in the rut of rigid thinking and acting."

Mark Devine – Sealfit

Some of the techniques I describe below can cause injury and possible death. Every aspect of safety in the practicing of these techniques has to be done with strict adherence to safety. There is never a guarantee of outcome for any self defense move in regards to injury to yourself or others.

I am not an expert in the field of hand to hand combat. However, I know that I have followed my personal philosophy for long enough to develop a certain understanding of defensive tactics. I have suffered through the hours of my own departments Defensive Tactics courses for almost three decades. I have studied the training and fighting philosophies of other disciplines such as MMA, karate, judo, and jujitsu. I participated in judo as a sport and I learned basic jujitsu once I became an officer. Having worked the street for almost 30 years, I have been involved in a number of fights. These always occurred as I was patting someone down, breaking up a fight, or trying to make an arrest.

There were several things that I always noticed at the conclusion of the fights. They usually went to the ground and the tactics from all of the training I received, never worked well against a subject who was actually fighting back or resisting. I learned that something else has to be taught. I know my own agencies idea of Defensive Tactics training is to incorporate certain aspects of ground fighting. The premise is right, but the reality is wrong. The people who partake in sport's like MMA are mentally and physically tough. However, there are problems training like an MMA fighter to use on the streets and it exist in the rules:

(Taken from the UFC website) The following actions are banned:

1. Butting with the head.

2. Eye gouging of any kind.

3. Biting

4. Hair pulling.

5. Fish hooking.

6. Groin attacks of any kind.

7. Putting a finger into any orifice or into any cut or laceration on an opponent.

8. Small joint manipulation.

9. Striking to the spine or back of the head.

10. Striking downward using the point of the elbow.

11. Throat strikes of any kind without limitations and including grabbing the trachea.

12. Clawing or twisting the flesh.

13. Grabbing the clavicle.

14. Kicking the head of a grounded opponent.

15. Kneeing the head of a grounded opponent.

16. Kicking the kidney with the heel.

17. Spiking a opponent to the canvas on his head or neck.

When observed, you realize that MMA is still a sport. These are many of the things that you will want to do if involved in a fight. All tactics apply if a subject decides to pursue a physical confrontation with the police. You are not paid to get hurt, injured, or killed. You are paid to protect persons and property from assholes. The martial arts self defenses taught are fine if you are in a competition. The entire purpose of the match is to place an opponent into a submission hold by following the rules that govern the sport. Training in real life to control or gain a submission hold on a subject that is fighting with officers, is exposing them to unnecessary dangers. Control and submissions are for subjects that are submissive or passively resisting, not grappling on the ground. Remember the FBI statistics we spoke about before; 25% of officers who ended up fighting on the ground were injured.

Compare the MMA rules to the target areas preferred by Krav Maga, the CQB of the Israeli Defense Forces: hair, eyes, temples, base of the skull, nose, ears, mouth, chin, jaw, throat, all four sides of the neck, clavicles, ribs, solar plexus, kidneys, stomach, fingers, testicles, thighs, knees, shins, ankles, and top of feet. The majority of these areas are soft tissue. Always target these areas with strikes and kicks in an effort to inflict the greatest amount of pain or injury with minimal effort. After a couple of well placed strikes, an officer will still have enough energy to maintain his security. More bang for your buck.

Follow through after these strikes with a transition to other weapons. There are no complicated grappling techniques which place you on the ground. Never try to stay engaged in some type of arm bar, neck lock, or wrist bend. Again, these techniques apply if a subject is actively fighting.

I like to learn how the best train and find ways to incorporate that training into what we do. I am not talking about other police agencies, although many of them are quite good. The downside to police training are the political correctness aspects that are incorporated for the legal defense of the department. The military does not worry about these issues in combat. I am talking about Special Forces Units. They train in CQB techniques or Close Quarter Battle tactics. They have spent decades studying the best ways to inflict injury and have had opportunities to develop these tactics in combat in the Middle East. One of the best things to come out of this type of training are the adjustments in battle tactics that give results.

Many of the units which operate in small teams, like the SEALS, Delta, and Green Berets, train to strike hard, fast, and evade. These tactics are essential to their survival because they are not intended for a long sustained battle. Apply this mindset to a police officer on patrol. Most of the actions we take are when we are alone. We are often out numbered and at a distinct disadvantage until our backup arrives. It is during these moments that I ask each of you to reexamine your practices. The job requires courage and calm nerves. Give your actions thought through mental preparations since fast reactions can save your life. Just as the Special Forces are required to train, so should we: strike hard, fast, and evade.

When has an agency ever required an officer to stand toe to toe with a suspect and fight it out, dragging each other to the ground in a test of strength, skill, or luck? This is why officers are given secondary weapons. Restraining a suspect who is passively resisting and then begins to actively resist requires officers to instantly adjust their mindset. This confrontation just became more serious because the subject can easily place you in a bad position on the ground. Get to your feet and deploy a weapon.

Most organizations initiated their training after the legendary Colonel Rex Applegate. Col. Applegate was tasked during World War II with training U.S. OSS agents. The OSS would later become the CIA. Applegate was to develop a system of fighting and training American agents during WWII. His techniques were found to be very effective.

Applegate had a few basic rules. He said that the training had to be fast, easy, and vicious. You cannot afford to spend years trying to perfect one of the martial arts. Besides, it is basically ineffective unless your opponent follows all of the rules of the sport. However, people who practice the martial arts understand the basics of striking and kicking.

Another rule was to always keep your opponent at arm's length by using your hands and feet. It is always a superior tactic to use any type of blow or strike rather than wrestle or throw someone to the ground. Strikes are easier to teach than the complications of a wrestling hold. However, once you go to the ground, never stop moving. Your single purpose from the ground is to get back up on your feet. If you are unable to roll, pivot on your hips and shoulders while keeping the suspect away with your legs and feet.

If the subject goes to the ground, it is not necessary for you to follow. The outcome could go either way if you are wrestling and an even greater danger exist should anyone join in with the suspect. When you are on the ground in a fight, the first person who resorts to blows, bites, and gouges will come out on top. Always attack the areas of the body that are easiest to hurt. If someone is kept in pain, they are unable to take the offensive. Again to stress the FBI statistics: 86% of confrontations ended on the ground, 25% of these officers were seriously injured, 12% were killed with their own weapon.

Do not forget the lessons learned in the Force Science Fatigue Threshold studies. This study found that your body begins to fatigue within 30 seconds when you are in an all out fight. In addition, you will exert more energy because of the extra equipment worn. You are wrestling on the ground with a subject who at first may be trying to escape. More energy is utilized trying to overcome than resisting. You begin to fatigue within 30 seconds and every second thereafter. Most people will experience almost total fatigue, especially in their upper-body strength after just two minutes. These times are dependent upon physical conditioning and were conducted with personnel who were in good shape. This should give everyone a reason to pursue a physical conditioning program. This also explains why 12% of injured officers were killed with their own weapon. Stay off the ground!

Let's assume you are in good shape as you sprint and tackle the fleeing driver from a traffic stop. You call out on the radio a quick "I'm in foot pursuit westbound towards … ." We have seen it time and time again. It is a natural instinct for most of us. We allow our ego and tombstone courage to take over. Besides, how many times have we conducted this same scenario and always arrested the asshole.

Because of the instant burst of energy expended to chase and tackle the subject, you are approaching the 30-second threshold of loosing energy. The subject is resisting, not fighting back. You are expending more energy than he is and starting to feel fatigued. What you do not realize is the passenger in the car has exited and is coming to the defense of his friend. There are drugs and a weapon in the car, and they both have served time in prison.

You are in serious trouble and your life is in their hands! This is not the way it was supposed to happen. You try to go on the defense, but there is another problem. Your energy reserves are almost depleted. In the distance, there is a siren of another unit en route, but audio occlusion has occurred and you cannot hear them. If you try to draw a weapon, you will probably loose it. Several officers each year are killed with their own weapon while engaged in this type of confrontation.

We will never know how this scenario finished, however, it concluded at the discretion of the bad guys. Your survival occurred at their liberty. What is their physical description after they flee? Who will the responding officers watch for? Because of your initial over response and lack of good radio information, you have placed the backup units in jeopardy. There will be no way to know if the people they encounter are the suspect's. The bad guys do not know that a minimum of information about them was released. They believe that they are being stopped for the worse thing they have ever done; the attack of the officer. There is an excellent chance that their next encounter will be as violent, if not worse.

Avoid going to the ground at all cost. This does not include handcuffing of a subject who is obeying your commands. If you need to kneel down to handcuff a person in a prone position, do it. Just be prepared to back off if they start to resist.

When punching, a closed fist is one of the worse ways to hit someone. You can suffer hand injuries like broken bones or the infection of a tooth cut or other problems. There is a reason why boxers tape up their hands and wear gloves; to protect their hands. Most people fight the same way they have always fought. Breaking out of the closed fist technique is difficult without practice. If you must practice striking with your fist, hit with the fist perpendicular to the ground and the thumb side of the hand on top. This is performed by not turning the fist and is like driving a joy stick. Another position is the rotation of the shoulder and arm where the top of the hand is facing up before impact. Without regular punching practice on a bag, hand and wrist injuries can easily occur. Our purpose is not to stand and box with someone, it is to strike quick and vicious to a vulnerable location. Remember what we said earlier. If you keep them in pain they cannot fight back. That applies to you as well. Imagine having a fractured strong side hand in a fight.

Remember the soft tissue areas discussed earlier? Open hands or hammer fist are the two accepted methods of striking. Most open palm strikes should be performed with your fingers extended and spread for palm rigidity. As for kicks, force is applied by using your entire foot while wearing shoes. Most people kick by striking only with the toe of the foot which applies less force. Regardless of method, any strike or kick at the moment needed is the best. Never become paralyzed with analysis. Strike the best way you can repeatedly and with as much violence as needed. Practice and mental preparedness will provide a plan of action in response to various situations.

In CQB training, the tactics taught are: hit hard and evade. The initial strike has to be calculated. Most of what we do must be quick and instinctive, which is where simplicity comes into play. There is one action that causes an immediate reflex response from someone: touching the eyes. As soon as someone grabs or starts to assault you, the first action will be to jab, flick, or sweep your fingers into their eyes.

If they bend forward as a reaction to this action, elbow strike them in the side of their head or knee them in the face or crotch. The golden spots for a knockout are the chin, temple, behind the ears, and back of the head. Cause a shock to the brain and the person goes out. A hit to the soft spots of the head with a palm strike will put them down. Touch your own soft spots on the head. The temple, under the jaw, top of the jaw behind the ear, and the base of the skull around the hairline on either side.

If the person goes backwards with the eye flick, step forward with a knee spike to the groin or a kick to the knee. For the spike, be sure to point your foot and toes back as straight as possible. This allows the knee to move forward as an effective strike rather than just up. A full foot kick on the forward knee can cause a serious and painful injury.

Another effective defense if they move their head back is to palm strike them under the jaw around the chin with your fingers extended. If the chin is tucked down, the nose or ears are also good targets. The nose can be struck just as you would the chin and the ears can be hit with cupped hands to force excessive pressures into the eardrums. Always take the first target of opportunity as it is presented to you. These targets can also be utilized in the event that you have been brought down to the ground by an assailant. Remember that your primary goal if you are down is to get back onto your feet. To repeat myself, the first person who resorts to blows, bites, and gouges will come out on top.

Remember the target areas for Krav Maga if the person tries to tackle you. A common method is the ordinary football tackle. They will go for your legs to force you backwards. This is the same technique used against Texas Constable Lundsford. After being knocked backwards, the other subject started kicking him in the the head. They removed his service weapon and killed him. As a defense, several responses could be a elbow thrust straight down into their back or leaning forward with your feet straight back to come down on top of the attacker. Once there, repeated blows to the kidneys will stop their advances. Then follow the first rule and get back to your feet. A technique to force someone off who is holding you down is to reach and grab their side skin in the area commonly referred to as the "love handles." Grip-squeeze the skin tightly. They will release long enough to allow you to strike at soft tissue. As they retreat from the pain, strike or jab them in the throat, eyes, kick them in their knee or crotch, or any other technique you can imagine.

These examples are very simplistic. In the real world, the only techniques which will work is simplicity. (I use simplicity as a catch word at the beginning of several chapters to demonstrate its importance.) I want to stress that these are options only in the event your life is at risk. These strikes must be repeated as many times as necessary to keep the suspect away. One sweep or jab may not work by itself; therefore, you must maintain a barrage of attacks to the soft tissue areas to create separation. You have to overwhelm them with jabs, gouges, kicks, and stomps.

Someone who grabs you straight on can be immediately reversed with a jab to the throat or eyes. Practice these simplistic moves as part of your situational awareness training. Shadow boxing or practicing on a punching bag will make you more efficient. When someone is trying to hurt you, do not try to restrain them. You will always be attempting to restrain someone if all of your training involves restraints and submissions. Train to strike, jab, and knee as hard and as often as you can to create distance. Remember to keep everything fluid. If one thing fails, keep trying various techniques to create separation.

Anyone who will intentionally assault a police officer is a dangerous person. It could be a gang initiation, mental illness, drug or alcohol abuse, or an ex con who has decided not to go back to jail. This person has already committed a felony. You have to assume they will cause serious bodily harm or worse if given the chance. How many videos have we watched where an officer is literally pummeled to the point of near death, brain damage, broken bones, teeth lost, and worse. Do not stand there and take it. Planning has to be fast and efficient. Perform any of these actions with even partial success and you will create the necessary distance needed to deploy a secondary or primary weapon.

Some rules can be definite, like stay off the ground. To get off of the ground; punch, gouge, bite, jab, knee, rip, tear, break fingers, or anything else you can think of. Be flexible with every situation. You are in a fight for your life. Stay flexible because no single technique will always work. Any training in self defense will better your odds on the street.

Study Train Survive

Summary of Hands On:

- MMA is one of the best fighting programs to simulate real life. However, there are many rules which govern the sport that makes it unrealistic.

- Real fights never occur as you were taught in your martial arts classes.

- When fighting for your life, grappling is the last thing you will want to waste your energies on. 25% of officers who go to the ground are injured.

- We are taught defensive tactics. To restrain a suspect requires offensive tactics. They will either try to get away (passive resistance) or try to cause you death or great bodily injury (aggressive or aggravated resistance).

- Your training has to be fast, easy, and vicious.

- Strikes, blows, and kicks are easier to teach and are more effective to practice than take downs, wrestling, and grappling.

- Always keep everyone at least at arms length.

- If you go to the ground, your priority is to get back to your feet.

- Try to roll out if you are on the ground. If you are unable, use your hips and shoulders to pivot. Keep moving and the first person who resorts to blows, bites, and gouges will come out on top.

- Remember the Fatigue Threshold Study; Upper body strength begins to fade within 30 seconds. Total fatigue in about 2 minutes.

- Palm strike using open hands to avoid hand injuries. Target soft areas with maximum pain infliction. (Eyes, throat, solar plexus, temple, crotch, kidneys, etc.)

- Kick using your entire foot instead of just the toe.

- Knee spikes – point your toe back so the spike moves forward, not up.

- Initial assault, target the eyes because they will cause an immediate defensive reaction.

- CQB targets the eyes, elbows to the side of the head, and knee strikes. The effectiveness is in the number of combination of fluid strikes and kicks.

- All of these strikes or blows have to be maintained repeatedly until separation is created. They have to be overwhelmed with the violence.

- Once separated, retreat and arm yourself with a weapon appropriate for the encounter.

- **Study Train Survive**

5 KNIFE DEFENSE

The best protection is self protection.

The best protection against a suspect with a knife is knowing they have it. Only then can you properly respond. If you know they have a knife, there are only two types of defense. One is to pull your firearm at the first sign of a weapon. The second is to try and escape to avoid the confrontation. There were two police officers killed in the line of duty in 2011 by knife attacks. This is a yearly trend and when I see several officers killed every year by a specific method, a chapter has to be dedicated.

If you are carrying a firearm, on or off duty, remember the importance of maintaining distance from an armed subject. A person can cover 30 feet in the average amount of time it could take you to draw and shoot your weapon. The FBI has shown that even with a well placed bullet in center mass, a person can still run up to 70 yards before the heart stops. A shot into the brain is the only one guaranteed to stop someone. In the chapter on firearms, we will discuss the need for instinctive or point shooting. Practicing these shots will assist in making a fast and accurate first volley; an absolute necessity to defend against this type of attack.

Most subjects will not approach with a knife if you draw a gun. Some will for various reasons from mental illness, drug or alcohol abuse, or suicide by cop. The foundation of this section is about reacting to an unexpected attack from a non gun armed subject. They may have a knife or blunt instrument, yet the defense will be the same. Create distance by whatever means possible. If the subject is too close, natural reaction will cause you to lean into the attacker to try and control them. However, to lean into a subject with a knife could result in an upper body strike and lead to your incapacitation. Practicing distance creation when confronted by a subject armed with a knife allows you the required time to draw and shoot. If they continue their advancement I can only say that life is about the choices we make while living it.

What if you are off duty or not in uniform? This means that you are not carrying many of the secondary weapons from a utility belt. The rule remains the same, create distance and protect yourself. If you have a gun, do not delay its use. Your life is in immanent danger. If you do not have a firearm, utilize whatever is available. A chair with all four legs pointing towards the subject is a good weapon. The assailant is not able to concentrate on defending against them all and you can use it in a thrusting manner. Strike with anything that can keep them away until there is an opportunity to escape. Never use your secondary weapons against an armed attacker if possible. This places you on unequal ground because unlike their knife or blunt instrument, your secondary weapons are not intended for serious bodily injury or death.

Some of the subjects encountered could be former military personnel. Additional care should be taken because they are taught tactics in knife fighting. Take the following various information which is directly from the U.S. Marine Corp Close Combat Manuel, Chapter 3.

"Marines experienced in offensive knife techniques can cause enough damage and massive trauma to stop an opponent."

"The goal in a knife fight is to attack the body's soft, vital target areas that are readily accessible (e.g., the face, the sides and front of the neck, the lower abdomen {or groin}).

Secondary targets are the inside of the thighs (femoral artery), inside of the upper arms (brachial artery), and the radial/ulnar nerves in the arms.

"Principles of Knife Fighting:

- Execute movements with the knife blade within a box, shoulder width across from the neck down to the waistline. The opponent has a greater chance of blocking an attack if the blade is brought in a wide, sweeping movement to the opponent.

- Close with the opponent, coming straight to the target.

- Move the knife in straight lines.

- Point the knife's blade tip forward and toward the opponent.

- Apply full body weight and power in each of the knife techniques. Full body weight should be put into the attack in the direction of the blades movement (slash or thrust).

- Apply constant forward pressure with the body and blade to keep the opponent off balance."

Thrusting of a knife means penetration. It is the most effective knife tactic because it can cause greater injury by damaging internal organs. Blocking with your arms means standing toe to toe with the subject and should only be attempted as a last resort. If your assailant is skilled with a knife, any attempt to block a thrust with your hands or arms, will result in damaging wounds. The psychological effects of blood loss could prevent you from maintaining a clear mind to determine your next move. Kick, kick, and kick some more, creating space until you can escape.

Although not as deadly as thrusting, slashing injuries are the most common and can have a devastating affect. If you are trying to defend yourself against a knife attack with your arms, a skilled person can easily slice you across the inside of your wrist, damaging the tendons and leaving that hand useless in your defense. Also a deep slash across the bicep muscle can disable the arm. If you are not carrying a firearm, escape at all cost.

There are a number of blocks, grabs, and parries (redirection of the incoming knife arm away from your body) shown in self defense practices as an option against a person armed with a knife. The self defense manuals I examined showed various arm blocking techniques. We have seen the demonstrations during martial arts exhibitions. The student approaches the sensei with a rubber knife and is told to do a slow overhead attack. The student approaches and follows the instructions. The sensei raises his arms at half speed to demonstrate the effectiveness of his skills. He blocks the knife arm of the student who suddenly stops the attack and cooperates with some type of arm lock, throw, or disarming technique. People are amazed at the skills of the sensei and cannot wait to be taught the same defense. A real attack is vicious and will not stop if you are lucky enough to get an initial block. Martial arts are most effective when the opponent is following the rules of the "art." Your best plan is to run. Never take on an armed subject unarmed.

The reason anyone ever uses a weapon is to gain the advantage over the other person. We have this mentality based upon our upbringing that fighting should be fair. We are taught the rules of a fight. We learn the rules that govern boxing, wrestling, martial arts, and mma. Even from an early age we would agree to meet in the back alley for a fight that was conducted within a learned set of rules. The truth is, there are no rules in a real fight. This is the idea we have to wrap our minds around. All is fair when it is a fight for your life.

In the last chapter, we showed the need to use every possible method to inflict pain and injury to an attacker. When a weapon is pulled, the attacker instantly becomes the greatest fighter of all times. Never take on an armed suspect unless you have a clear shot. In a real fact based scenario, the knife wielding attacker is not going to wait and move in circles with you while waiting for the best opportunity to slip through your defenses. They are going to rush you. When this occurs, all of the martial arts training in the world is not going to keep you from getting hurt. Their intentions are to kill you. As you read at the end of almost every paragraph, your best chance of surviving this encounter is escape. No amount of martial arts rehearsing will ever place you on equal grounds with this person.

Always make sure you can see the palms of their hands. An effective method by a trained person with a knife is to hold the knife in the ice pick grip. They will have the knife blade pointing up the back side of the forearm with the cutting surface pointing out to their rear. When close enough, they will punch with a hook technique allowing the cutting edge of the blade to pass forward and across your face or neck. They will stop immediately and reverse with a thrust to the neck or chest. Always know where their hands are and what is in them.

Colonel Rex Applegate said, "Either type of knife defense, parry or block, involves a certain amount of risk." He also taught classes in knife fighting tactics. He developed his own design which was about 10 inches long, shaped like a dagger. The Applegate knife has a round handle, swollen in the middle for the placement of your middle finger and a double edged blade. This type of blade prevents anyone from grabbing the knife. This knife was carried by both American and British agents. Techniques were developed in assassinations of enemies of the state during the war. In his book, *Kill or Get Killed*, Col Applegate demonstrates numerous ways of killing with a knife from sentry guards to crowded streets.

According to Col. Applegate, the signs of someone skilled with a knife are: they carry the knife with the handle in their palm, blade protruding forward with the edges parallel to the ground in front of their thumb and forefinger. This allows the attacker to sweep the blade left or right to slash the opponents arms in any attempt to defend themselves. The knife is kept close to the body and their weak hand forward. This arm is used to create the needed opening to thrust the knife. Knife selection is also a consideration. Most inexperienced persons will grip the knife like they are holding an ice pick or hammer. The hammer grip is only good for an upward thrust and the ice pick for a downward thrust. Knife defense techniques were developed for these standard grips. They are the commonly seen methods on movies and demonstrations because they appear dramatic. However, they are ineffective.

Col. Rex Applegate demonstrating proper knife grip and stance.

There is a timetable for death as demonstrated by W.E. Fairbairn for the survivability of a cut artery. W.E. Fairbairn trained the Shanghai Police in the 1920's up until WWII. He was brought back to England to teach Special Forces Units techniques in hand to hand combat. Colonel Rex Applegate was one of his students for a train the trainer course. Fairbairn was an expert in knife fighting. It is said he was covered with scares from being engaged in so many knife fights. Though the information in the chart may not to be exactly correct, it does give you an idea of the dangers of a cut artery.

EXPLANATION OF FIG. 112

No.	Name of Artery	Size	Depth below Surface in inches	Loss of Consciousness in seconds	Death	
1....	Brachial	Medium	½	14	1½	Min.
2....	Radial	Small	¼	30	1	"
3....	Carotid	Large	1½	5	12	Sec.
4....	Subclavian	Large	2½	2	3½	"
5....	(Heart)	—	3½	Instantaneous	3	"
6....	(Stomach)	—	5	Depending on depth of cut		

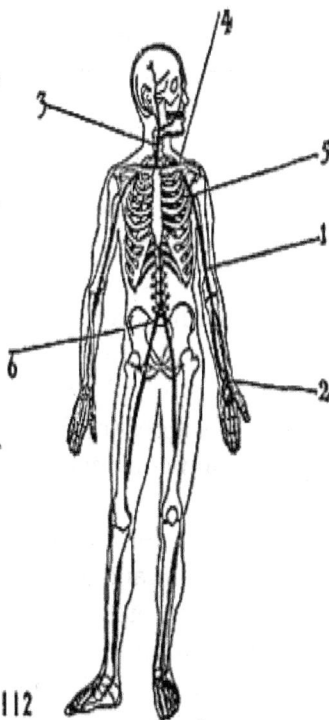

Fig. 112

(This chart is courtesy of *Get Tough* by W.E. Fairbairn)

I have always stressed the importance of determining if a subject has a criminal record because they are inherently more dangerous. Most stabbing methods are developed and perfected in correctional institution's. Watch prison videos and see how fast these attacks occur. They come straight in, fast, and stab repeatedly. Also watch how their intent to attack is always shown in advance through their body language. Everyone demonstrates behaviors of their intentions. Knowledge of a criminal record should always cause a heightened sense of awareness. We learned earlier that 73% of the subjects who ran from the police had a prior record. Never underestimate the dangers involved to police from a multiple offender facing enhanced prison time.

Remember that there are only two actual defenses against a knife attack. Use your firearm or create distance by running. If you are unable to do either, kick hard and at good targets to maintain the needed distance in order to prevent the knife from causing damage in your torso, neck, or head; and then run.

The charted times above are for when no medical assistance is immediately available. Some injured areas are impossible to stop bleeding. Proper first aid kits and survival information is available to all in law enforcement today. How many officers carry a tourniquet to stop bleeding? It could be an injury to you or a fellow officer. Have you ever thought about what to use like a belt or a shoelace? These will work if you think about and take the time to retrieve them. My suggestion is to always wear a para-cord survival bracelet. If you or someone else is seriously injured, the bracelet can come apart and be used as a tourniquet. You can use them with or without a buckle. I prefer the knot over the buckle bracelet because it is the original design and easier to cut or break apart if needed. Some of these bracelets are more decorative rather than designated for survival. I prefer the bracelets constructed of a single cord instead of the designer multiple lengths. They can be difficult to find, however, any of them will work. Cut off the knot and the bracelet is easy to unravel. They are available everywhere, including my website at: criminalinterdiction.yolasite.com

Study Train Survive

Summary of Knife Defense:

- There are only two types of knife defense, a clear and effective shot or escape.

- If you are unable to do either, keep the assailant away from your vital areas with the use of kicks.

- A knife instantly makes an opponent the most dangerous person in the world.

- Always be sure you can see their hands and what's in them.

- A person can cover 30 feet in 2 seconds. Remember your reaction time to shoot.

- Even after shot in an area of great blood loss, a person can still run up to 70 yards.

- A brain shot is the only shot from a handgun which has stopping power.

- Maintaining distance by whatever means or the use of anything as a weapon is your best opportunity to survive if you are unable to run.

- Understand the dangers of a military trained subject because they have basic knife fighting skills.

- A skilled person with a knife is demonstrated by the way they carry it in their hand. The classic hammer or icepick carries are learned from too much television. A blade protruding forward with the blade sideways, weak hand up, and the knife held close is the proper stance. This person is dangerous.

- You must avoid your normal self defense tactics and understand that you are instantly in a life or death struggle the very moment a knife is brought out. Take the necessary action needed to save yourself.

- Plan ahead with first aid ideas for yourself and others as well. In a knife assault, slashing injuries are most common. A tourniquet may be needed and can be readily available with a para-cord bracelet.

- **Study Train Survive**

6 FIREARMS TRAINING

The decisions you make when faced with destiny will determine whether you live or die. It simply comes down to taking the correct action in a swift manner.

Shooting practice should never be considered target or defensive shooting. For law enforcement and the safety aspects of this book, it is about shooting effectively against an armed assailant. You have to be able to use your firearm instantly and accurately. Our goal is offensive style training in instinctive, point, or combat shooting. This technique stresses the fast use of the handgun without the sights.

Law enforcement personnel are losing nearly 70% of their gun battles. In *Criminal Interdiction,* I described it like this; "Most police involved shootings occur no further than 21 feet (81%). 58.8% of all police shooting occurred from 0 to 5 feet. In fact, the FBI's "Law Enforcement Officers Feloniously Killed in the Line of Duty" research from 1994 to 2006 showed that law enforcement officers failed to hit their assailants 69.4% of the time."

Police officers are trained in the basics of pistol craft and targeting skills. They learn to take a moment for sight picture, sight alignment, breathe, and trigger squeeze. This traditional style of shooting in order to meet your department's range qualifications alone, fails on the qualifications course of the street. As with many training courses, additional aggressive styles of combat shooting has to be practiced. Force Science Research has shown in their gaze assessment studies that only learning the basic shooting techniques are getting police officers killed. The reasons why the assholes win more often varies. First and foremost, they are not on a restrictive course requiring them to shoot regularly in only basic pistol shooting styles. We will perform as our training dictates. Police officers are trying to engage in fast shootouts by doing exactly as they are trained; sight picture, sight alignment, breathe, and trigger squeeze. By the time they reach the sight alignment phase, the assailant has fired. Now the entire process is interrupted and panic sets in as our shots become uncontrolled. If your assailant has military training, they have already been taught to fire fast and keep their eyes on the target. I have the same complaint today that Col. Rex Applegate had about the training received by law enforcement since the 1940's. Basic pistol craft and some stress course shooting is all that is performed. There is no combat style fast shooting. We are teaching our officers defensive training, bulls-eye paper target practices for competition and setting them up for failure. The proof is in the statistics.

Point or instinctive shooting was developed as a natural response to an armed encounter. In a close shooting scenario, you have to fire fast and accurate. There will be no time for the standard sight alignment rules. At close range, you will be shot if you delay or miss. Instinctive shooting relies on all of your natural responses to these dangers with more control.

If you train to shoot where you look without the gun sights, your chances of surviving will increase dramatically. Think how many police shooting videos you have watched where the officer starts shooting until the magazine is empty and still they miss the bad guy. After the proverbial smoke has cleared, there are scattered casings from both sides on the ground. If anyone is shot at all, statistically, it will be the officer. Force Science Research has shown that if you take your eyes off of the target to focus on the sights, the chances increase to miss and get shot first.

Actual photo courtesy of www.bobtuley.com

Photo is a freeze frame from the famous Kehoe Brothers traffic stop in Ohio. Armed militiamen versus Ohio State Trooper and deputy in an all out gun battle. The deputy and subject on the right of the photo emptied their guns at one another. Shooting as trained, no one was hit, even at this close range.

Every police officer begins their training in the academy. They are taught the basics of pistol craft to pass the qualification course. This is a necessary continuum in the progression of firearms training. You have to be familiar with all of the functions and maintenance of your handgun, train under various conditions of stress to learn how to fire on target, and how to steady the gun on various support items to assist you in making an effective shot.

Under stress, your heart will be pounding, adrenaline flowing, and hands trembling. The shot needs to be steadied to be on target. You can become proficient with fairly long shots with your handgun when you learn to use the sights correctly. This standardized training and other point style shooting techniques requires more time on a range than will be provided to you by your department. Training is one of the first areas to be cut when budgets are reduced. As I said in *Criminal Interdiction*, "the cost and time necessary to develop these skills rest on you."

I have heard this time and time again: "If the agency is not going to buy it for me, then I must not need it." This is the common call of the complainers. It is up to YOU to take the additional steps needed to complete the number one rule in law enforcement; Go home safe at the end of the day. You are going to have to spend the money and time to go to the range. This idea of shooting your gun during your annual or bi-annual firearms qualifications course and not pulling it out of the holster again until the next course IS COSTING LIVES! If the reason is being too cheap, then keep all of the receipts for expenses and you may be able to use them as a tax deduction.

I really want to stress to everyone the need for a full and balanced training regimen in the use of firearms. I am also quite aware that most officers will never try to accomplish more with their firearms training than what is afforded by their department. These are the same officers that will be your backup. I have my own opinions on how to train those who want to improve their firearms skills. I am a certified firearms instructor and have taught pistol craft for my agency for a very long time. I can teach you how to shoot with a proficiency to qualify. Teaching you how to win in a gun fight is a totally separate endeavor.

As we mentioned in the beginning, this is combat, instinctive, or point shooting. Nearly 60% of gunfights are going to occur within five feet. The person who can fire first and with accuracy is the one who will walk away. We can be on the defensive, but not shoot with a defensive attitude. Do not wait until a subject has fired before taking the initiative to fire back.

In the Force Science Gaze Assessment Study, the rookie cops delayed in drawing their weapon until nearly a second after the suspect turned on them. The elite trained officers had drawn well before the suspects pivoted against them and fired their weapons first in 92.5% of the cases. The rookie officers fired first only 42% of the time. In addition, the rookies took their eyes off of the assailants in 82% of the scenarios in order to try and achieve a sight picture. This action essentially removed them from the gunfight causing them to miss most of their shots. They were responding exactly as they had been trained with defensive target practice style qualification shooting techniques. They knew as they entered this scenario that something was going to happen and still failed.

Even though this study utilized rookie officers, I am sure that most veteran officers would have the same results. Most of us were never trained for this type of action. It is dumbfounding that agency heads and training personnel do not recognize the need for this realistic style shooting. We need to be proficient in both areas of practice. After a qualification course is completed, a stress course can be conducted along with instinctive shooting and fast draw practices. Fast draw practices can be conducted with dry firing for safety purposes. How often do you see officers on the firing range hang up in their holsters while trying to draw their weapon? How can you expect to quick draw in a real gunfight if you do not practice fast draws? Create a little more distance and then bring the gun up to eye level. Fast draw to a hip shooting position is a common range practice, yet the accuracy of this method is poor beyond point blank range. Speed and accuracy will help you win in a shootout along with the following techniques.

The first concept of instinctive shooting is that you do not utilize the sights. Imagine being in a low light or no light situation or someone pull's a weapon on you during an encounter. It is often called instinctive shooting because the process involved is instinctive. Imagine the handgun as an extension of your hand. Right now as you read this, quick draw your finger. That's right, pretend your hand is the gun and look around you. Fixate on any object be it a clock, television, or painting. Now draw your hand as the gun and your forefinger as the barrel and point your imaginary gun quickly at the fixated object. Keep your eyes on the item. Look down to see how well you are sighted in. You will be surprised at how simple this is to learn. The same process is followed with the handgun except now your hand and finger are replaced with the grips and barrel. Practice this procedure with a safe gun (always double check that the gun is empty and the chamber is clear). Repeat the process numerous times until the action becomes second nature. Now you are ready for the range.

Start at the 3 yard line and follow the natural process from the draw to the shot. Practice this method repeatedly until you become comfortable and never look at the gun sights. Pay attention to the placement of the rounds and forget about the perfect quarter size grouping. You are trying to hit the target. Never over-think the process and just let your muscle motor skills do this naturally.

Square up on the target with your weak side foot slightly ahead. Face forward in a crouched position. This allows for several things to occur. First your body armor is directed to the front to protect you from a hit in center mass. In the Weaver position, which stresses a sideways stance, exposes the side gap in the body armor and your arm pit to the shooter. A round taken into these areas can have fatal consequences.

The second advantage to being squared off with the target is your ability to move. You can walk or step in any direction with an almost natural gait. When walking with your gun on target, your gait should be adjusted. A natural walking pattern involves too much body movement. To smooth this out, think about your heel placements and the distance of each step. When you are walking with the gun at eye level, each step will intentionally be a soft heel to toe roll of the foot. This allows for forward body movement without the up and down causation's of a natural gait. In other words, you will be able to maintain a steady eye picture (not sight picture) on the target.

You should practice with a very tight grip on your handgun, even if it is different from what you are normally accustomed. The reason is when faced with the type of pressures involved in a shooting, your muscles will naturally tense with the stress of the events. This grip can affect your accuracy; therefore, practicing a tight grip now will pay dividends later if you are involved in a shooting.

It is always better to move the gun position up from a low ready than a high pointing location (the Hollywood version of holding the gun next to your head with the muzzle pointing up). From the high position or close to the chest, the gun will be thrust forward, but there is a tendency to shoot low. The natural angle of the wrist along with the frame design of some pistols (revolvers do not have this same frame issue) causes the barrel to point downward at the end of the thrust. From the low ready position, an almost locked elbow prevents thrusting the gun out when brought up to shooting level.

When the gun reaches eye level it should be on target and level. Pull the trigger without hesitation. Keeping the gun in the center of your body and shooting from eye level, you will shoot where you look. If your subject is at an angle, do not move your arms to them, pivot your body. By turning your body towards the target, you maintain the gun in center mass. Maintaining eye contact with the mark assures you will be on the objective instantly as the gun rises. Swinging your arms around, instead of turning your body, can cause the shot to go wide.

Another interesting topic is in the number of shots fired. In most standardized firearms courses, we are given a set of instructions and a time frame like, "For the next course of fire, when the targets turn, shooters will draw to a two handed high point shooting position. Shooters will fire two rounds in four seconds. Shooters will then maintain cover until told to re-holster." At a different area of the course you will be allowed to shoot 12 rounds in 45 seconds. This is fine for the firearms qualifications course. It does not prepare you for the realities of a gunfight.

According to the FBI's firearms training unit. Most gunfights will last anywhere from 2.5 to 3.5 seconds. During this time it will require at least 3.5 shots to stop an assailant. These are shots that the suspect takes to the body. We also learned earlier that a suspect can run up to 70 yards after receiving a shot which severs a major artery.

The answer to this puzzle is in your training. You have to learn to draw and fire fast and accurately. You want four or more shots to their body in three seconds. A well placed head shot is the only one that will take anyone down immediately.

I hope you are beginning to understand the importance of instinctive shooting. When most people are delaying their first shot to aim, you have already fired with a reasonable chance of striking the target. When they are trying to align their sights, they have taken their eyes off of you. You have fired and are firing again causing them to react defensively and panic causes their shots to miss. Keep your arm extended, elbows locked, and fire as fast and accurately as possible while seeking cover. With a minimum of practice, this method can be counted upon to save your life. It does not take an excessive amount of time or ammunition to become proficient. Simply practicing with your hand and finger allows the exact pointing position to become second nature.

The accuracy of this method begins to drop at distances greater than 15 yards. Therefore, practice instinctive styles at varying yardages inside this range. In addition, most range courses are drawn out from the 3, 7, 15, and 25 yard line. To help with your proficiencies, also choose yardages which are between these marks because every shooting will not take place at these exact yard markers. 81% of all police shootings have occurred within 21 feet; the same distances you are practicing.

Another area of concern is the use of our shotguns or rifles. Once or twice a year, while at the range for qualifications, we will participate in a shotgun familiarization course. Fire a couple of rounds at a target after trying to load or combat load a certain number of rounds. Occasionally, you may have a course which will cause you to transition between the shotgun and handgun. In other words, few law enforcement personnel spend much time training with their long guns.

The basics of loading, unloading, stance, shoulder placement, safety, grip, and target acquisition can be stressed. Low recoil shells can resolve the high recoil complaints against using the shotgun.

Additionally, proper grip with the push pull technique can be demonstrated. As you prepare to shoot, push forward with your weak hand harder than you pull with your strong arm and this will reduce much of the recoil. This also helps you to stay on target rather than trying to realign after bringing the shotgun down from its high recoil position.

Some advanced techniques can be shown after everyone successfully completes the basics. Areas like selective ammunition loading, weapon retention tactics, and transitioning to your handgun. This is another strange truth that has always amazed me. We practice the least with the shotgun, yet it is one of the most efficient weapons we carry. Additional use in various situations can change the stigma that many people have with shooting a shotgun.

The same philosophy can be applied for the use of a rifle. Many officers today are carrying an AR15 rifle which they have taken a dedicated course before being allowed to carry it on duty. The problem then becomes the same as the shotgun. Once or twice a year you are required to fire a couple of rounds at a target to qualify. The gun is cleaned, encased, and placed back into the car. Additional training is necessary for the safe operation of the gun. Without regular use, the operations of the weapon like the safety/fire selector switch, clearing jams, and magazine reloads are not automatic. Hesitations will always put you on the receiving, rather than the giving end.

The .223 cal bullet is a very good round to use inside of a home or building. This will be explained as many of you are squirming over the belief that it is too powerful to use inside because of collateral damage to innocent bystanders. In the next chapter, I will show the importance of correct weapons selection. Tactics for the use of the gun in these confined areas need to be rehearsed. We have learned in Iraq and Afghanistan that our troops are constantly climbing in and out of vehicles. They are also conducting building sweeps and raids on compounds. The same actions transfer cleanly to the warfare at home through law enforcement operations and presented several safety issues which were addressed by various techniques.

The Army has specific training for this style of operations because it is the standard current warfare model. They call it MOUT or Military Operations on Urban Terrain. This came about as warfare shifted from rural to urban operations. First is the length of the weapon inside smaller rooms and vehicle interiors. The second is the extra care needed to prevent soldiers from sweeping others with their gun muzzles. By short stocking, the adjusting stocks assist in both of these issues. By keeping the stock shortened, it reduces the length of the gun. From inside the vehicle, this allows easier access in and out and also when the use of the gun is needed from within to fire out.

When you are moving through a building, if you shorten the stock, the gun is usable in the tight confines of a room. Other than some practice with a reduced stock, there is no difference in shooting techniques. The gun can remain on your shoulder for natural and accurate target acquisition. Eyes on target and point shooting techniques are of the utmost importance, not sight alignment. There are other methods of short stocking that take the butt of the rifle off of the shoulder. To stay within the model of simplicity, I feel nothing beats a normal shooting style. Different carry and shooting positions can cause hesitations. Every shooting technique I have described, is from a normal and natural shooting position. Therefore, they can all be taught easily with effective outcomes. Besides rapid target acquisition, accuracy is imperative and the most accurate technique to fire a rifle is with the stock against the shoulder.

Study Train Survive

Summary of Firearms Training:

- When practicing with your firearm, stress both the targeting of your shots and combat shooting techniques.

- Almost 60% of police shootings occur within 5 feet of their assailant. Law enforcement fails in nearly 70% of their shooting encounters.

- You are personally responsible for your own safety. Your agency will teach the basics, you have to get to the range and practice yourself.

- When training yourself, emphasis must be on instinctive combat shooting.

- Keep your eyes on the target, not your sights.

- Practice quick draws with a safe weapon. Practice these same quick draws and fire at the range.

- The technique involves a fast draw from a low ready or holstered position. The gun is brought up to eye level and fired.

- Walk deliberately with a rolling heel to toe gait.

- Keep the gun square with your body and on the target. Therefore, the gun will be on the target when it is brought up to eye level.

- Pivot the body and not your arms when the target appears at an angle to you.

- Be proficient with the operations of your long guns. With an AR15, practice firing the weapon with the stock in it's shortest position. Shooting from the shoulder is still the most accurate firing position.

- **Study Train Survive**

7 GUN AND AMMUNITION CHOICES

"Giving up is the ultimate tragedy."

Robert J. Donovan

There are some agencies wanting to replace the shotgun for many of the popular patrol rifles. Though they are very similar in function there is a place for both of these weapons in your arsenal. I would like to demonstrate when and why you would prefer one over the other.

You often see a police officer with an AR15 over their shoulder on the news. The environment where they are utilizing these weapons should be the determining factor. Would they be better off with a handgun, shotgun, or rifle? For handguns, there are several schools of thought. There are the small and fast groups vs. the large and slow. They both carry facts behind them, however, after reviewing numerous ballistics data comparisons from private testing to the FBI, several things remain in the forefront. You have to hit the suspect in center mass. The bullet has to penetrate deep in order to hit anything vital or there has to be vast tissue damage. There are many misconceptions about handgun cartridges. An important truth about the handgun ammunition is there is no such thing as knockdown power. Critical to this information is the fact that there is enough oxygen in the brain to conduct further actions against you for about 10-15 seconds after the heart stops.

Surrounding tissue damage occurs from the kinetic shock and fragmentation of the bullet. Tissue damage can also occur from the expansion of the bullet itself. The problem is that fragmentation will only occur if the bullet is in excess of 2000 fps at impact. All of the handgun ammunition's are below this velocity requirement. These are velocities which occur with rifles. Therefore, fragmentation combined with the greater kinetic energy tissue expansion occurs when hit with rifle bullets.

With handgun ammunition, a permanent cavity (the cavity created by the bullet itself) is formed and a temporary cavity is made by the kinetic energy. Human tissues and organs have great resiliency to shock waves which is why handgun ammunition leaves only a temporary cavity. The temporary cavity is momentarily expanded around the permanent cavity, yet returns to its original shape. The damage is caused by the permanent cavity that may be increased by bullet expansion. The size of the permanent cavity conversely corresponds to the size of the bullet. A .38 cal +P hollow point bullet can leave a permanent cavity with the narrow entry neck and an expansion end to approximately .59 inches, as long as the bullet expands. A .38 cal bullet is actually closer to a .36 cal and was so named for the size of the chamber that was needed. The 357 mag is closer to the actual size of a .38 which is why it can be fired in the magnum. This is about a 63% bullet enlargement from impact to the point of rest. Compare this to a shotgun slug or a Foster slug from most police smooth bore shotguns. If the slug does not expand, there is a 1 inch permanent cavity created by the bullet. This is a lot of damage depending on how deep it penetrates. With all of this in mind, do not jump on the hollow points and expansion train just yet. The idea is sound, but is the reality of bullet expansion all that important?

A .223 cal bullet at around 3000fps creates a tremendous release of energy and fragments on impact. The combination of the two forces stretches the permanent cavity so far and fast that tearing and rupturing of the wound channel, which was weakened by fragmentation, causes a significant increase in damage. This is typical of a rifle wound.

We spoke about the .38 cal bullet expansion. It is essential in understanding wound mechanics that handgun bullets are not dependable in their expansion abilities. There are two key components to having an effective handgun cartridge. The bullet has to penetrate enough to strike vital organs for blood loss and it has to be big enough to leave a large permanent cavity. Remember, handgun ammunition is not fast enough to allow for effective fragmentation. Expansion and penetration also varies from different makes of the same caliber. Not every manufacture creates an equal bullet.

In an attempt to try and resolve this problem, the Glaser Safety Slug was developed. It was touted as the great man stopper and safe to use in your home. The bullet was designed to be frangible so as not to penetrate walls. The selling point was that on impact, the bullet disintegrates and there is a transfer of shot to the body causing devastating damage. The problem was significant superficial damage, but shallow penetration; which violates the first effective requirement of a handgun cartridge. Forensic scientist stated that after being shot with a Glaser Safety Slug, it would take about three days to die and the cause would be by infection. Thus the cartridge eventually lost its popularity.

Forensic scientists have determined that there is very little difference in the permanent cavity when comparing hollow point to solid ammunition. In fact, hollow point handgun ammunition has been shown to only expand in the body 60-70% of the time. If the bullet impacts anything before striking tissue, it can fill the hollow point and prevent expansion. This includes striking clothing as the material can wrap around the bullet. You will see in some of the following test how this can cause a deeper penetration.

The length of the gun barrel as well as the brand and type of ammunition's used can have significant changes to the bullet velocity. Kinetic energy is energy possessed by an object in motion. Energy is a function of mass and the velocity squared or $E=MC^2$. For our purposes, our energy is possessed by a projectile or bullet in motion. The longer or further this bullet is in motion, the less energy it possesses. The bullet can also sustain a loss off momentum upon impact along it's trajectory. The important factor of this energy is that enough of it has to exist to deliver an adequate amount to the target. Too little energy, and the bullet does not have enough to transfer to the target. Too much and the bullet passes through the target with limited transfer. The goal is have enough to penetrate and stay in the body so that there is a complete energy transference. This is why a .223cal bullet is so effective. It is traveling with a great deal of velocity which correlates to energy. Upon impact, the speed causes a fragmentation and total energy transfer. The combination of the two equates to a lot of damage.

Longer barrels give the propellant more force and time to work on propelling the bullet. At some point, if the barrel is too long, friction begins to play against the bullet. The key is to find an appropriate length. With rifles, a 20-22 inch barrel is sufficient. If they are magnum or heavier loads, 24-26 inch barrels increase the force-related energy and allows the bullet to achieve it's needed velocity. For handguns, revolvers commonly have large barrel variances. Although impractical, the ideal length for maximum energy in a revolver is a 16 inch barrel. Having a four to five inch barrel with a revolver is the ideal length in both power and practicality of use. There can be as much as 150 fps (feet per second) loss in bullet velocity per inch of barrel. A 2 inch snub-nosed .38 will have about 300 fps less bullet velocity than a 4 inch barrel. The same for the .357 magnum comparing a 3 inch to a 5 inch barrel. The standard pistol barrel of between four and five inches seems ideal for most of the ammunition's used. For more information on barrel lengths, read the Ballistics By The Inch web site. They do very detailed studies on these and varying ammunition types.

According to FBI forensic scientist, the critical components of effective ammunition are penetration and permanent cavity, in that order. A bullet must be able to penetrate the human body at least 12 inches, though 18 inches is the preferred depth. These penetrations are needed to reach the vital blood bearing organs. Increased bullet mass can increase penetration and in a gun fight, you will want every available advantage. Big caliber cartridges fire the largest bullets which will cause the most damages; as long as there is a minimum of 12 inches of penetration.

The size of the gun caliber has to be considered for the second component of effective ammunition: permanent cavity. Never buy handgun ammunition based upon it's ability to expand because this factor is not dependable. Additionally, the permanent cavity shows no difference between a hollow point and solid ammunition's. Again, as with penetration, the greater the mass of the bullet corresponds to the size of the permanent cavity. However, if the bullet does expand with enough penetration, there are added probabilities of the projectile touching an artery or vital organ. They are all statistical possibilities, but again you should take every advantage allowed.

Both Winchester and Speer conducted ammunition testing at the Burbank Police Departments Firearms Training Center. They fired standard ammunition from a handgun, rifle, and shotgun slugs into bare gelatin to simulate human tissue and then through interior wall material before bare gelatin. The results were as follows:

Average Penetration in Bare Gelatin

.40 S&W 180-grain Hollow Point	16.0 inches
5.56mm 55-grain FMJ	11.0 inches
12-gauge, one ounce slug	21.0 inches

Average Penetration through Interior Wall into Bare Gelatin

.40 S&W 180-grain Hollow Point	25.0 inches
5.56mm 55-grain FMJ	06.0 inches
12-gauge, one ounce slug	21.0 inches

If you examine the first chart of bare gelatin, the greater penetrations are from the slower handgun bullet and shotgun slug. Remember, increased bullet mass can increase penetration. The 5.56mm or .223 begins to fragmentize on impact and will definitely spread damage by velocity energy transference exasperated by fragmentation. Because of the additional fragmentation and expansion of damage from a .223, we are not concerned with the reduced penetration. Deep penetration is only essential in handgun ammunition or sub 2000 fps rifle ammunition.

Examine the second chart where each round was first fired through an interior wall before striking the bare gelatin. The shotgun slug has the same penetration. The 5.56mm began to fragment as it hit the wall and penetrated less into the gelatin. The .40 cal hollow point actually had a greater penetration than the first test without the wall! The hollow point filled with wall material and failed to expand, thus penetrated deeper.

Another test was conducted by Olympic arms in Washington State. Their test mirrored that of the Burbank test results.

Caliber	Testing median	Penetration	Condition
.223	gelatin only	9.5"	two pieces
.223	wall & gelatin	5.5"	fragmented
.40 S&W	gelatin only	13.5"	mushroomed

| .40S&W | wall & gelatin | 22" | no deformation |
| 12 gauge slug | wall & gelatin | 27.5" | mushroomed |

When inside of a house, very little is going to slow or stop that 1- ounce shotgun slug from hitting someone (The same goes with handgun ammunition). Despite what many think about the over penetrating power of a .223 caliber cartridge, the truth is actually the opposite. If you take these ballistics test and apply them to the real world, the .223 caliber bullets are safer for use inside of a home. They also provide precision and quantity of rounds going downrange at the target. The same could be applied to "00" buckshot. The nine pellets from "00" buckshot provides an effective pattern for the short standard shot distances faced within a house.

Some agencies are discussing whether or not to stop issuing buckshot. Because of its standard shot spread of about 1 inch per yard, buckshot only has an effective range of between 25 and 30 yards. Some say it is much farther, yet through a smooth bore police shotgun; effective shot placement is questionable beyond this range. A shotgun slug can have an effective distance of about 100 yards. It will have an average gravitational drop of almost 5 inches at this distance. It will hold almost true at 50 yards. Therefore, for those who really want a rifle, you can have an excellent medium range rifle with your shotgun.

In a standard law enforcement patrol environment, if you are issued a 12 gauge shotgun, it should be fully loaded with slugs. However, I do believe that every officer should have "00" buckshot available. These extra shells can be carried in an elastic shell pouch on the shotgun stock or placed in a cartridge belt to throw over a shoulder. If you have to enter a home, transitioning to buckshot is a better ammunition to cover the close quarter battle or CQB environment that this scenario presents. In addition to the shotgun, if your agency allows officers to carry rifles, the AR15 is very effective.

As we have seen, the .223 cal rounds are safe inside a building or home and would definitely assist in reducing the risk of an accidental "friendly fire" incident. For rural patrol officers, it will also give you the ability to reach out to a suspect in open country. In testing, the .223 will penetrate a windshield or door of a car. However, as we have come to expect, the bullet will begin fragmentation and energy loss on first impact. The difference is the rapid multiple round capability and range of the gun.

I said at the beginning of this chapter that there was no such thing as a measurement of knockdown power with handgun ammunition. There are some newer hunting caliber handguns like the .50 cal and even larger designs in production. These guns fire a tremendously large bullet which could cause greater damages than our standard weapons. However, most test only include the ammunition's which are feasible. The .45 ACP is the largest used in regular testing. The larger magnums like the .44 and above are too difficult to control to be an effective fighting weapon. Handgun ammunition does not actually have the ability to stop you in your tracks and drop you unless you are hit in the head, shutting down the central nervous system. We have been mentally trained to drop to the ground when shot because this is what is seen on television. We have mentally crippled ourselves into believing that every gunshot wound is fatal. This is far from the reality of an actual gunshot wound. According to the U.S. Centers for Disease Control and Prevention, between 1993 and 1998, there was 114,600 incidents of gunshot injuries. Of this total, less than 31% were fatal.

The FBI's Firearms Division actually tested the impact of a 9mm and a .45 ACP. They measured the muzzle velocity of each and compared the energy to a one-pound weight and then a ten-pound weight. The results showed that a one-pound weight dropped from a height of under six feet would equate to being shot by a 9mm. The ten-pound weight would have to be dropped from a distance of .72 inches. For the .45ACP, the one-pound weight would have to be dropped from a height of just over 11 feet and the ten-pound weight from 1.37 inches for equivalency. As you can see, neither of these have the actual ability to knock you down. The knock down comes from our own mental disadvantages.

This demonstrates the importance of a positive winning mental edge so you can fight through the injury and survive. Understand that if you are shot, the odds are in your favor for surviving the incident. For others who fall into that defeated status, "I have been shot, I am going to die" attitude, may simply will themselves to the "light." I have always said that success in this job is as much mental as it is physical.

As for off duty carry, studies show it is best to carry the same or similar gun as your on duty. This is the weapon that you are familiar with and utilize the most. You have had the opportunities to clear jams, reload, and draw. Many officers carry a completely different type of firearm when off duty. I agree with this only if you are very proficient with many hours on the range with the gun or an equally designed model. An example of this is if the Glock model 26 is your on duty weapon and the model 27 as off duty. They are both functionally identical.

If you do carry an off duty gun, it is imperative that you also carry extra magazines or speed loaders. We have already seen how often we miss in the violent explosion of an armed encounter. The ability to reload is as important as carrying the gun itself. One without the other is a definite risk to your life.

As far as our on duty weapon, most everyone is restricted to carry their department's gun. For those who still tout the effectiveness of smaller cartridges, I can only go back to the testing. You may be able to carry more rounds per magazine, but the essential elements lay with the damage done when you actually strike the target. Yes there has been more people killed by .22 cal LR ammunition than any other in America. However, that has to do with the cost and availability of the cartridge, rather than the power. The issue is placing a firearm in your hands that provides the greatest opportunity to stop an aggression, not if it can kill. Larger is always better. The single most important factor in handgun ammunition is penetration. Having a gun without proper penetration capabilities has caused the lives of officers. I again stress that you should never buy ammunition for its ability to expand. The greater mass of the bullet will increase the penetration as will the design. Hollow points may or may not be the best option. Explore the various manufactures of ammunition because they are not all the same. My advise is that we will get back from something what we put into it and this includes the cost of ammunition. Based on penetration and permanent cavity as the known factors of effective handgun ammunition, bigger is better and wins the argument.

Study Train Survive

Summary of Gun and Ammunition Choices

1. Educate yourself with the science behind ballistics.

2. If you are able to, carry a large caliber handgun.

3. Never buy ammunition for its ability to expand.

4. The two determining factors of effective handgun ammunition is penetration and permanent cavity, in that order.

5. Any caliber cartridge can kill; you need effective penetration from a heavy bullet and multiple hits to vital areas to ensure that the assailant is stopped.

6. Most shootings have shown that it takes at least 3.5 hits to stop someone. Practice firing in groups of four or two sets of double taps.

7. .223 caliber rifle ammunition is a good choice for rural patrol and building entries. With the stock shortened, the length of the weapon will be no more than your extended hand with a handgun.

8. Shotgun slugs are excellent for medium ranges up to 100 yards. They have tremendous penetrating abilities and should not be considered for building entries. A 5.56mm or "00" buckshot are better alternatives.

9. Hollow point handgun ammunition will fill or wrap itself in any material before striking tissue. Even without this expansion prevention, hollow points fail to expand in 30 to 40% of the cases.

10. A positive mental attitude will assist you in continuing the fight.

11. When off duty, carry the same or very similar weapon as when you are on duty.

12. Always carry extra magazines and/or speed loaders.

13. Study Train Survive

8 OFF DUTY/PLAIN CLOTHES

"The mystic bond of brotherhood makes all men one."

Thomas Carlyle

I write about this topic for a very simple reason. In 2011, there were four police officers killed by gunfire while off duty. Included were three officers (one of them from the off duty status and two plainclothes officers) who were shot and killed by other police officers! This is actually a yearly average not a sad single event. What the hell is happening here? One problem is the mentality of off duty officers feeling a need to intervene in crimes in progress. The other problem is in the poor procedures of identifying yourself as a police officer.

Whenever you are off duty, any situation you encounter has to be evaluated as to the importance of your involvement. There are many factors that have to be considered. Many of us have never discussed, much less mentally prepared for these situations. Therefore, when they do occur, reaction to them is the same as if you are on duty. However, you are not on duty and not easily recognized as a police officer.

According to the FBI's Law Enforcement Officers Killed and Assaulted or LEOKA reports, from 1975 to 1985, 130 off duty police officers were feloniously killed. In the three years of 1991 to 1993, 35 officers were feloniously killed while off duty. Almost half of these occurred when the officers tried to intercede in robberies. Often times, off duty officers tried to intervene in a robbery when they themselves were unarmed. Other times they tried to intervene when there were multiple suspects. In each of these situations, the odds are stacked against us.

When an officer is off duty, they are not properly equipped to handle criminal situations. They may carry a handgun, but how many carry extra magazines, handcuffs, radio, secondary weapons, body armor, or a radio. In addition, there can be confusion in the minds of other officers arriving at the scene as to your identity. Great care needs to be taken in the decision-making of the off duty officer who witnesses a crime. Are you with your family at the time? If so, could your actions place your family members in harm? What are the policies of your own agency? Even the simple act of stopping to assist disabled motorists have had its tragedies. Recently, an off duty officer was struck and killed and another was stabbed to death while trying to change a tire for someone else. In addition, you do not have emergency lighting to warn approaching traffic to slow down. Sometimes it is best if you pick up a phone and call it in to the proper authorities. There was a time when it was alright to pick up hitchhikers and stop to help strangers on the road. Today is not that time as morals, values, and respect is a thing of the past. Be smart for yourself and love ones.

Put yourself in the shoes of a responding on duty officer who arrives at the scene of a violent crime in progress and they see you holding a gun. At that very moment, what separates you from the criminal in the eyes of the officer? Several off duty officers have been shot and killed by responding officers when the bad guy dropped their weapon and the officer stood there with their gun. We are trained to never surrender our weapon. In our mind, we know we are the police and did not think to drop the gun. In the mind of the responding officer, they only see someone holding a gun which makes you an immediate threat to themselves and others!

I am not saying that you should never take police actions while in an off duty capacity. I am saying to place more thought into these actions than if you were on duty. The difference is in whether or not your inactions could be as effective as your actions. Many times while off duty, your best option will be a good witness. Unless you or another persons life is in immediate danger and you're in an armed position to take action, being a good witness is the best offensive. Think about what to do in this type of event before it happens. Are you armed? Do you have additional ammunition, your credentials, badge, and identification card? Is the act you are witnessing an immediate life threatening event? If you observe a property crime like theft, burglary, or even a robbery, try to be a great witness. These events can easily escalate into violence. Even if the asshole is unarmed, without your secondary weapons, you are on equal ground should they resist, a position I have preached about avoiding.

If 911 is contacted, be sure to notify the operator that you are an off duty officer with a description of your clothing. Tell them everything about the events, suspects, victims, and yourself to inform the arriving officers with as much information as possible. This may sound ridiculous, but several off duty officers have been killed by uniformed officers over this lack of communications. If the responding uniform officers tell you to drop your weapon, immediately follow their orders. Advise them you are a police officer and the location of your credentials, but do not reach into your pockets or take any action which could cause them to take further actions.

When you are on duty and working in a plainclothes assignment, be aware of your appearance when responding to events. Just as in the off duty capacity, many on duty plainclothes officers do not have all of the necessary equipment. They should have some type of outer wear identification like raid style jackets or vest. Take for instance a recent event of a armed man call in an apartment building. The first officers on the scene encountered a man with a knife who attacked them and they shot and killed the suspect. You can only imagine the adrenaline rush of the officers on scene and the responding officers tensions as they listen to the events unfold over the radio. Responding officers want to get there as fast as possible. Immediately after the gunfire and the suspect goes down, a uniform officer sees a man running with a rifle towards the front door. He immediately thinks it is another suspect and opens fire. The man is shot in the chest and dies at the scene. He is a plainclothes detective running to help his fellow officers. He has no vest or other markings to identify himself as an officer and failed to realize how his personal appearance would affect the others on the scene.

The solutions to these events are fairly simple. We have to think about the consequences of our actions in advance. We have to remain calm and remember when we should and should not be involved. Follow the procedures laid out by your own agencies. Failure to do so could lead to personal civil liabilities. We sometimes have to learn to be a great witness to create a safer environment for all. Control your actions and concentrate on the suspect(s) to assist the responding officers. This is the same scenario seen in the Foot Pursuit Chapter. Excitement and over reaction can lead to a poor physical identification. The on duty officers will have to face additional dangers of not knowing the correct description of the suspect. The last thing we need is unknowingly facing off with another officer. One can only imagine the strain of having to live with the actions that led to the injury or death of another officer.

Study Train Survive

Summary of Off Duty/Plainclothes

- Be very up to date on your own departments' policies about your responsibilities when off duty.

- Understand that when off duty, you are not properly equipped to handle most scenarios.

- Try some mental preparations for off duty situations to assist with a controlled response. These preparations should include understanding the off duty requirements of your agency, the type of crime, are you equipped for the event (extra magazine, clear and proper identification), and is it a life threatening crime. Property crimes should never be intervened.

- Try to resist that police officers urge to instantly jump into an event.

- You should in most cases, unless it is an imminent life or death situation, try to be a good witness for the on duty officers. Nearly half of the off duty officers killed occurred while trying to stop a robbery.

- When you pull your weapon without a uniform on or without proper identification, think how another officer would respond seeing a civilian with a gun.

- Remember you are not on duty. Follow all instructions given to you by the officers on scene.

- Several off duty or plain clothes officers are killed each year by on duty officers.

- **Study Train Survive**

9 BUILDING ENTRIES

"The absolute pacifist is a bad citizen; times come when force must be used to uphold right, justice, and ideals."

Alfred North Whitehead

Patrol officers are frequently called upon to enter homes, offices, and buildings. There is nothing routine about a building search. Tactical teams have the advantage of practicing these entries during their regular training sessions. I was assigned to our SRT (Special Response Team) for over a decade and received good training from various sources. The advantage of being assigned to these specialty units are they will routinely train with other agencies. It is here officers can see advancements in equipment and tactics used by others. I am writing this section for the patrol officer, but not to exclude officers with tactical training.

As with many of the things we do in law enforcement, entering a building alone is never recommended. There are too many areas of concern and points of ambush to consider. In certain areas of the country, some agencies are so small that many of the officers are lucky to have backup. However, the reason for the entry has to first be decided. Call in a tactical team if you know there is a person inside with a gun. They are better equipped for these types of operations. Different approaches can be made depending on the type of call you are on. You and your backup can complete calls of non violent crimes that requires the home to be cleared.

The initial decisions to be made are: what type of entry is being made, what are your objectives, and compare the objectives to the risk. Once this is determined and the decision is made for the entry, be sure to have an advance meeting. I do not care how many times everyone has worked together, meet in a neutral location and discuss the plan of action. This can be as simple as a brief talk to a detailed operational plan.

The majority of actions I was involved with were drug warrants. Others included arrest warrants, and knock and talks. For the street officers, you will be involved in investigating calls for service. An alarm has sounded and you need to clear the structure or the scene of a 911 call and be advised that the suspect is still inside the house. The first course of action is to determine the type of crime involved, whether a weapon was involved, where that weapon is now, are there any other available weapons including firearms in the home, and how many suspects could be inside.

Next, try to gather as much information as possible regarding the layout of the house, any other suspects or victims inside, and the last known location of the suspect. Be sure to have enough officers to secure the scene and enter the home. Notify a supervisor of your plans and follow all of your departments' rules in these actions.

If needed, two officers can cover the homes exterior. Positioned at a corner of the home opposite of one another, two sides can be watched at the same time. Be sure you watch your zone from a position of cover or concealment. Once the home is secured on the outside, how to enter can be decided. Entry into the home should be through only one location to prevent any cross firing.

The house will normally be entered through an open door, however, try to use every possible access point to your advantage because the suspect will also concentrate on the doors. Try to gather some intel through quick glimpses in a window that exposes the room you are going to enter. A good extension mirror, used to search vehicles, can also be utilized. Avoid the windows if the house is dark as street lighting or simple moonlight can easily silhouette you. Again, if you believe there is an armed subject inside, avoid all windows and call for a tactical team.

The first aspect of the entry is a quick ingress and seizure of the property. Determine the size of the room to decide on the number of officers needed. For a standard home, a clear and search team of two officers per room should suffice. Placing more officers in these small areas can cause them to bunch together while trying to maneuver around the common furniture. At least one or two officers should follow the initial team. This first phase is the control phase. The officers need to make entry and rapidly secure any visible suspects. The military model of entry is acceptable. This is where the first two officers enter through the fatal funnel (so named for the area where the officer is silhouetted in the entry point as seen by anyone in the room) and turn left or right to cover the sides. The third and fourth officer can move forward, yet out of the funnel. These forward moving officers should not over step their side covering distances being provided by the first and second officers.

The first officer will move in and away from the opposite side of the door which is hinged or the side with the door handle. The second officer can then move in the opposite direction of the first. The initial officer, if they move in and to the right, should cover everything in the right quadrant of the room. The second officer who is moving into the opposite side of the room covers the other quadrant. The side officers need to maintain their attention to the sides to protect everyone else entering the structure from side fire. Many times a suspect will move to the sides of the entryway. If all of the officers move rapidly forward, they will pass this suspect who will then be in a dominating position behind the officers. Once inside, if there is no area to the side to cover, like a wall, move forward at the pace of the team to cover any approaching areas to your side of the room.

With the main area cleared, the teams can move toward the other rooms. The lead officer can "cut the pie" to each room before entry. By watching "slices" of the target room and sweeping past to see all angles, assures there is not a suspect in a position of ambush. Once completed, the two entry officers can enter the room. The one or two other officers can cover the unsecured areas until the entry team retreats from the room. The two officers who enter the room, should immediately enter left and right out of the fatal funnel again. Once the main areas are cleared, they can initiate covering techniques for a more definitive search of the room.

Care should be taken when opening closet doors and cabinets because they are also fatal funnel areas. Your baton or other device can be used to open these from the side while the other officer is covering from the opposite end of the room. Do not bunch together and keep talking to a minimum. Noise control is important for making it difficult for the suspect to know exactly where you are in the house. Always enter a structure with a flashlight, even in the day light hours because the areas searched are usually dark. Once the room has been secured, the search team can reenter the hallway with the cover officer(s) and repeat the process again until the structure has been secured.

This has been a quick overview of the basic processes involved in this type of action. It is imperative to discuss and try to obtain at least annual practice on the current techniques of structure clearing. Definitive instructions need to be in place for officers as to when to call in a tactical team and/or supervisor. If any of these instructions are contrary to your agencies directives, always follow the departments' policies. However, if anyone feels a specific policy should be readdressed, they should take action through the appropriate chain of command. It is not about right or wrong, it is about safety.

Study Train Survive

Summary of Building Searches

- Determine the nature of the entry and whether it should be conducted by a tactical team.

- Determine the size of the structure to be searched to ascertain the number of officers needed.

- Have an advanced plan so everyone understands their specific role.

- The exterior can be covered with a minimum of two officers on opposite corners.

- Simple entries should be made by three to four officers. The military option is acceptable with the first officer in moving opposite the hinged or the door handled side. The second to the opposite direction of the first. The third and fourth moves in and forward, yet out of the fatal funnel of the doorway. These officers have to be careful not to over advance their side cover. The side officers are to cover the sides until clear to advance.

- Rapidly clear the areas for any suspects in plain sight to secure the premises.

- Have the lead officer "cut the pie" at all doorways to assess the open areas of the rooms.

- No more than two officers to enter each room. One to search and the other to cover. Additional officers maintain cover of the unsecured rooms.

- Stay out of fatal funnels which include all cabinets and closets.

- **Study Train Survive**

10 BEHAVIORS/ATTENTION/AWARENESS

"Our lives are defined by millions of tiny decisions and only a few big ones. We tend to focus on the big ones, but it is the tiny decisions that stack up over time and define who we are."

From Sealfit by Mark Divine

I included these topics together because you cannot read one without being aware of the others. We all know about learning to read body languages, voice commands, and responses (all of which I will discuss), but attention? Attention or our attention to detail is a very important aspect of officer safety. Attention is how the brain operates when receiving all of the information in our surrounding environment. Think about the various mental distractions we have to work with each day. Our brains can only focus on one thing at a time. That one thing is the only thing that we can focus our attention on.

Despite how good we think we are at multitasking, we are really only good at one thing at a time. When we think we are multitasking, our minds are actually switching from one activity to the other. There are many who believe they are excellent multitaskers. You can drive, watch the calls on the computer screen, listen to the patrol radio, and talk on the cell phone. In reality, your brain is only programmed to handle one of these situations at a time. When you are involved in one, the others are not getting any attention. You say to yourself, "but I am on the phone all of the time and driving while watching the calls on the computer." Yes you are, just not at the same time. Think back to when you were trying to read the notes on the computer and talking to someone on the cell phone. One or the other actually gets cut off for that moment as you switch your attention between the two. Then suddenly, you have to brake hard to avoid a collision because your attention to driving was also turned off. When we have been driving for many years, the actions we take are more reactionary. You do not have to think about when to brake, accelerate, or turn the steering wheel. They are simply trained motor skills. Accidents occur when you do not notice to take the action in time.

The brain is simply unable to focus on everything; therefore, it tries to prioritize the most important. What it considers important at that moment may not be the most important thing to you. Additionally, if you're thinking about other things you will not be able to focus. Attention is like a spotlight and you will only notice the objects in the light. If you spotlight on one person, no one else will be noticed. This is the inherent danger of dealing with multiple suspects. When they are out of the car or as pedestrians, you cannot deal with them all.

Keep everyone in their cars until a situation arises that requires them to be out. When dealing with multiple suspects deal with one and make the others stay away. As additional officers arrive on the scene, direct them to focus on the others. Recently, in central Florida, an officer was shot in the head and killed while patting down three suspicious subjects. He knew back up was on the way and failed to wait. We have all done the same thing many times before. This is NOT criticism of this fallen officer. It is a harsh lessen for the rest of us. When trying to do multiple things when dealing with a suspect, you will only do one thing right. This one thing will then be something else, then something else, and so on. If you will remember this simple fact of attention it may one day pay off in saving your life. Remember the FBI statistics from the first chapter. 38% of officers were killed during a crime in progress. 60% of those officers were killed while trying to make an arrest of the suspect before backup had arrived.

Attention can be controlled by distraction or misdirection. One person could start going through their wallet, which will focus your attention. The other suspect recognizes that you are concentrating on the item and pulls a weapon or discards contraband. If focused on something, you may not notice other things that are happening.

In order to prevent this, stand back and control the encounter. Do not move close and wait for back up. By standing back and not focusing attention to a single person or object, you are keeping your attention on the entire chain of events. The moment you start reading drivers licenses or writing notes, your attention is now misdirected from the overall situation. Make sure they keep their hands out of pockets and in sight.

This brings up a fascinating reality called inattentional blindness. The brain is simply too overwhelmed with everything in our environment. Therefore, we have attention to keep us focused on specific items of interest. Remember that we can only focus on a single event. To allow this to happen, our brain ignores everything else. Because of this normal psychological event, large things can occur around us and we never see it happen. Think of magicians when they have you concentrating on one thing while changes occur in the background. They are not expected and your focus is directed; therefore, you will not notice it. You may not always notice change where it is not expected. This is a common cause of motorcycle accidents. We look down the road before pulling out from a side street. We take a quick glance. Our mind is focused on cars, vans, trucks, etc. The motorcycle, bicyclist, or pedestrian approaching is literally removed from the vision. The accident occurs and we are left telling everyone, "I looked and never saw anything. I have no idea where they came from."

The same psychology applies to law enforcement. Knowing how this "change blindness" occurs, train yourself to focus on a series of events. For instance, you are about to stop a car. Training teaches us to watch the people inside the car and their behaviors like: how the driver operates the car, where the driver is looking, the brake lights and turn signals, how they pull off of the road and stop their vehicle. Can you watch all of these things at once? From a distance, your center of attention is the car. As you focus on more specifics, create a checklist of things before, during, and after the stop. If you mentally follow this checklist of indicators, then one by one, eliminate them from the list. You catch up to the car and do not immediately activate your emergency equipment. You observe the driver and passengers. What are their behaviors like? Is the driver watching you in the side and rear view mirrors? What about the car, is the license plate proper? Now is the time to run the tag, not after the stop. Are there air fresheners, bumper stickers, rental car signs, or other things that could heighten the event?

In your mind you have mentally check listed the occupants and the car itself. Activate the emergency equipment and proceed with the traffic stop. Does the car stop immediately or travel some distance before stopping? What are the occupants doing? Did the car stop a safe distance from the road? Are you stopping about two car lengths back from them? Are the brake lights and/or turn signals still on?

You can see how placing the item into a mental checklist allows you to safely conduct the stop. Most officers will see the car and make the stop. They may notice a couple of the items, yet miss many more. There are just too many things to observe at the same time. The ones missed could have been the signal needed to save your life.

Attention redirection, is a phrase we probably play with more than anything else. A pick pocket artist will be good at redirecting your attention. They get you to look at one thing while they concentrate on taking something else. Magicians and illusionist do the same thing. "Watch the cards," they will say which focuses your attention. Once that has happened, they can do most anything else they want. Keep in mind that attention is single topic focused. If your focus is where someone does not want it to be, they will cause a distraction to redirect your attention. Remember the Lunsford tape out of Texas? He has two subjects out of the car while searching the trunk. There is no way to watch everything they are doing. They distracted and then rushed him. In Alabama, an officer is talking to a driver he has stopped about his speed. The driver, who has a bad attitude, mentions his brother is a police officer. The officer asks for the brothers name and number. As he takes his eyes from the driver to remove a note pad, the driver shoots the officer in the head. An attention redirection was added which caused the officer to be distracted. This is a case I write about at length in my upcoming book, *Criminal Interdiction II*.

Suspect behaviors tell all if you can maintain your attention to the details. It is like developing a baseline. You have experienced hundreds of different people during the course of your job and developed a baseline for normal behaviors. When you come across someone behaving completely different, take notice and investigate. It is kind of like animal behaviors. Domesticated animals like to interact with people. They are curious and trusting. Wild animals never want to get close to humans. They are not curious and live in a constant state of fight or flight. Given the chance they will leave. Left with no options, they will fight. This is the same with criminals and the average person. Normal people have no problem being around you while the crook wants to stay away.

I have talked about this topic in every class and book. Body language or Kinesics is the study of nonlinguistic body movements. We all have behaviors that will exaggerate under pressure. Just as a polygraph machine measures changes in blood pressure and heart rate, so can you. These changes cause a person to sweat and adjust behaviors. Start watching everyone's behaviors when you have them stopped. Pay attention to their breathing, their pulse rate in the neck, the pulse in their suprasternal notch, their hands and what they do with them. The standard for a resting heart rate is 60 – 100 beats per minute. If you are out with someone and you have back up present, ask them if you can check their heart rate. Check the brachial pulse in their arm, or if they say no, simply watch the pulse rate in their neck. Count the number of beats in 10 seconds and multiply that by 6. This will give you an approximate heart rate which will help you to determine how stressed they are.

Do their hands shake, but relax as the encounter progresses? This shows how they are calming down in your presence and therefore not feeling guilty. Watch as they look through their wallets and purses. Do they tremble, try to hide the contents, or start to look and then stop to say they do not have what it is you have asked them for? Pay attention to their eye movements and the direction they are looking. They will often seek a way out or towards your weapons, their car, their accomplices, etc. Observe their inability to stand still while asking them questions. Look at the items which are in plain view around them. They can tell a lot about the habits of the person. Is there Visine or lighters in the console or seat next to them? Ask them if they smoke. People keep close the things they use regularly. Why have a lighter immediately available if you do not smoke? Chapter 9 of *Criminal Interdiction* is dedicated to this topic.

There is one behavior which I believe is the single most important an officer can watch for, audio occlusion. When you have to repeat your commands, be prepared. The person is beginning to shut you out because their mind is becoming occupied. They are redirecting their focus internally and we can only focus our attention on one thing at a time. The internal thought processes are unlikely for anyone confronted by the police. They are entering their fight or flight, over stressed, adrenaline pump. They are very scared and are mentally trying to decide the best course of action for themselves.

In almost every video of an officer being assaulted or killed, you will hear the officer repeat themselves to the suspect at some point before the attack. It may occur only once, but you will clearly see the behavioral change of the suspect. Just as you are paying attention to the video, pay attention to your suspects. Avoid distractions because this is when they will initiate their actions.

Situational awareness is a topic we need to be reminded to keep it in the forefront of our minds. It is about taking stock in your surrounding environment. You have to be aware of the areas and the people in them. When stopped and writing reports, be cognizant of the area you park, the accesses and blind spots, as well as looking around frequently for anyone approaching. The largest, empty lot makes a good place to park so you can see 360 degrees around. Do not wear your seat belt to allow for a quick exit if needed. Several officers are killed each year from having someone approach and shoot them. The same precautions have to be applied while in restaurants or other businesses. How often have you seen the events of a deranged gunman entering a restaurant or other establishment and start shooting everyone? Sadly, it is a common occurrence around the world. Remember that there was three police officers murdered as they sat in their cars while not involved in any specific police duty. They were simply in uniform and presented a target.

In *Criminal Interdiction,* I described situational awareness as: "Be aware of your surroundings at all times. I already know that this not completely possible all of the time. But just like your traffic stops, everywhere you stop should be considered. As you pull into a parking lot or an abandoned area to work on reports, be aware of the area. When walking into restaurants or convenience stores, do you survey what is going on inside before entering? Do you sit at a restaurant in a place of advantage or disadvantage? Wild Bill Hickok was killed while sitting at a table with his back to a door. Recently in Washington State, four police officers were shot to death while sitting at a table and working on their computers at a coffee shop. Situational awareness is everywhere you go on or off duty. You should park in an area where you can leave easily and it is well lit. The area where you park should have a clear view all around. This is so you will not be surprised if someone approaches you. Remember, with the technologies that exist today in a patrol car, like in car computers, it causes us to stare at the technology all of the time. Be aware of your surroundings at all times."

Sports psychologist and top Olympic coaches use visualization techniques for their athletes. It is estimated that 90% of Olympic athletes use some form of visualization and 97% say it helps. Visualization techniques can also reduce stresses and builds confidence. It helps you to focus on doing important things right and is proven to help when the actual task is performed. The mental imaging initiates the repetitive muscle responses which will place the action into your normal motor skills. You can see why this simple mind practice can make a difference in your survival.

When alone, practice visualization techniques involving various scenarios. Have them in mind during a traffic stop or another type of encounter. Quickly in your mind say, "If this person does A, I will respond with B. I can follow B with C and D if necessary." Plan in your mind for the various types of events that can happen. Therefore, if it or something similar does occur, you will automatically respond with planned motor skills. This instant reaction can mean the difference for your survival.

Maintain mental awareness regardless of your agencies actions. What I mean is this is a job of offensive measures despite what your department's political correctness bureau advocates. Job safety depends upon your swift decisions and actions to problems. A good cop is one who is aggressive. They seek out the criminals, not wait for the next call to come in from a civilian. Do not fall into a defensive mindset. Maintain the offensive and take the fight to them.

Agencies bowing down to public opinions based upon political correctness have hurt and killed officers. We do not have to wait for suspects to hit, kick, grab, resist, stab, try to run over, or even shoot before you take action. This entire idea of defensive tactics is ridiculous when you consider that our job is to restrain and arrest which can only be accomplished through offensive tactics. To protect life and property does not mean to sit and wait for them to take the first action. You have to take the initiative or offense to keep yourself safe.

In 2011 there were four officers who were killed in ambush style attacks by gunfire. Many more were ambushed and not killed.

You have to remember that this world is a dangerous place. Your destiny will be equivalent to how well you are prepared. Not all evils can be prevented, but situational awareness and visualization techniques can help.

Study Train Survive

Summary of Behaviors/Attention/Awareness

- Despite how good we think we are at multitasking, we are all simply doing one thing at a time.

- Attention is like a spotlight. We see only what is in that light when we give it our attention.

- The environment is too complex for the brain to take in everything so it developed attention to help.

- Our attention is single focused and is why dealing with multiple suspects is so dangerous.

- Inattentional blindness is the focusing of the brain and its inability to see everything around it. This is why we fail to see large objects in front of us.

- One way to avoid missing important items during repetitive or complex events is creating a mental checklist. Events like traffic stops can be broken down into a series of individual items that you can check off in your mind. Advance with the checklist as the stop progresses. This keeps the list from becoming too large to remember.

- Suspects will often try to create an event which will cause your attention redirection. It is one of the inherent dangers of dealing with multiple suspects.

- Study Kinesics in any format possible. I discuss the topic and behaviors in my book, *Criminal Interdiction*.

- Watch people's heart rates when you are with them. 60-100 beats per minute is the average for a normal resting heart rate. Significant increases can indicate over stressed.

- Beware of audio occlusion when dealing with people. Any time you have to repeat yourself or are ignored, extreme caution is advised. They have mentally blocked you as they try to find a way out of the situation.

- Always be cognizant of your surroundings. It does not matter where or what you are doing, always scan around for unusual activities.

- Visualizations is a simple self tactic you can use to mentally prepare yourself for a variety of occurrences. This mental planning will also lead into your motor skills for a faster reaction.

- **Study Train Survive**

11 **THE END OF THE SHIFT**

"There is a destiny that makes us brothers, none goes his way alone. All that we send into the lives of others comes back into our own."

William Jennings Bryan

I always finish my books with a chapter called, "The End of the Shift." This is the pentacle of each day. Success can be measured by how we are, both mentally and physically, when our shift is over. I truly believe that this outcome rest squarely on our own shoulders. There will be events which will happen by the grace of God, however, we do control the outcome of most. The best we can do each day is plan, prepare, pay attention, and react. It is all part of my idea of the **Study Train Survive** philosophy.

We have to take our personal care into consideration each and every day. We have to take the time to eat a healthy diet, participate in an exercise routine, and have regular check ups. Last year alone, nine police officers died of heart attacks in the line of duty. We are concerned over the number of ambush gunfire deaths, shocked by the number of officers shot and killed by other police officers, saddened by how many officers were killed during pedestrian encounters, and upset by the number of officers murdered during foot pursuits. The problem is, when taken separately, each was equal or less than the number of officers who died from heart attacks.

Post retirement, the life expectancy of a police officer is from 5-15 years less than the general population. We also have one of the highest divorce rates at 15-25 percentage points higher than the national average. Our suicide rate is DOUBLE the national average, and we own an alcohol abuse record higher than most any group.

It has been scientifically proven that the job of law enforcement is the most stressful job in America. Some of the primary reasons for this stress is the use of your firearm, the on duty death of a fellow police officer, shift work, and dealing with the problems of the world. To add to this, in my upcoming sequel to *Criminal Interdiction*, I will be covering a topic which is being proven as one of the great stressors of all; human confrontation. Human confrontation or as I have always enjoyed saying, asshole confrontation is our job. We have to take care of ourselves first and foremost. If we do not, we will never be able to take care of others.

One simple thing we can do at anytime is breath control. It may sound strange to some, but I have used this with success. It is a valuable tool and can have a dramatic impact in a multitude of areas. Breath control helps to reduce tension which can activate adrenaline. It focuses your mind and thoughts by reducing the amount of stress which can be externally applied. In other words, it helps you to remain calm under pressure so your mind can make better decisions which can affect our destiny. Deep and slow, inhales and exhales, can help you achieve the right decision without the emotional explosions of a fight or flight response. However, should the events call for action, make yours swift and with the amount of violence needed to overcome.

Our mental and physical health has to be taken into consideration as to when you should retire. Not everyone is able to deal with the stressors of this job in the same ways. For myself, in the last years of my career, I discovered that I was developing hand tremors. Concerned, I had these examined and tested repeatedly over time. The end result was muscle tremors due to stress. Now I have learned that three other Troopers I used to work with have developed Fibromyalgia. One is trying to retire while burning off all of his leave, one has filed for disability from his current agency and the other is just beginning the painful and debilitating symptoms. All of these guys are in their 40's. In addition, I have learned the hand tremors I had developed are very common with other officers. Many try to hide their symptoms out of fear for some type of agency retaliation.

Several possible causes are believed to be that serotonins are released from the brain to relax the central nervous system during stressful events. Eventually these chemicals are reduced from overuse and the body fails to control pain properly. Stress causes too many fight or flight incidences which eventually causes excessive nerve firings in the muscles. These are most pronounced in the hands. Whatever the cause, everyone one has to remember that we are in daily combat in the streets of America. Having this grind for 20-30 years can be excessively brutal on our systems. Add to this the difficulties of everyday problems and you can see why divorce rates are the highest. To try and deal with these issues, many officers turn to alcohol. Do not forget that marital discord is the primary cause of police suicides. The outcome is the combination of 24 hour a day stress applied to a person who finally snaps. Those of us who complete our full service time have to learn to entirely reprogram ourselves. This is a job of adrenaline highs and lows which cannot be compared to any other, yet few of us would have ever done anything else if given the chance.

I included at the end of this book two additional Appendix's. They are the Fatal Errors and Fatal Errors of Law Enforcement. They show the problems that can lead every officer into danger and the most common errors that directly led to their death. Everyone has at sometime seen these list. It is apparent these simple list has not yet sunk in with us. Read them again and be reminded.

I ended my last book with the following paragraph. It leaked some personal feelings from my soul at the time as I knew the end of my active career was coming to an end. Now, less than a year after I wrote this, I can confirm just how true it is.

"In the end, when you are tired and ready to give it all up, it will be your family who is there waiting for you. The day after you leave, the job has already forgotten you. Life goes on no matter how important you think you were. Did you make a difference? All of the things you accomplished throughout your career did make a difference to people you will never know. Someone was saved by your actions somewhere. No one may ever know this, but you. I said it at the beginning and will say it again in the end. The job entails more than most realize and produces a brotherhood that few understand. It is that self satisfaction that we will all feel, at the end of the shift. "

Study Train Survive

Appendix I

My Classes

Florida Highway Patrol Academy

Search and Seizure x4

DEA Narcotics Investigative School

Surveillance Techniques

Domestic Marijuana Eradication and Aerial Identification School

Advanced Criminal Interdiction School x7

Commercial Motor Vehicle Interdiction School x6

Instructor Techniques x2

DEA Drug Interdiction School

MCTFT Advanced Drug Training

US Customs Cross Designation x2

First Responder

PR24 Instructor x2

Auto Theft Investigators School x2

Investigative Interviews x2

Firearms Instructor

Fiber Optics Operations

Survival Spanish x2

Courtroom Testimony

Interviews and Interrogations Instructors School

Advanced Investigative interviews

FTO Certified

In Car Camera School

Contraband Interdiction Instructors School

Mini Buster Certification

Drug Prosecution Course

Dignitary Protection School

Israeli Instinctive Shooting

Mental Arms Training

Powerful Presentations School

Laser Operators School

US Treasury Drug Enforcement Investigative School

Trucks and Terrorism

Rural Patrol Drug Investigations

CMV Criminal and Terrorism Interdiction

K9 Handler School

Islamist Cultural Awareness and Terrorism

Incident Response to Terrorist Bombings, Basic Bomb School

DEA Meth Lab School

Patrol Rifle School x2

ICE Crossover Training

Street Gang Investigations

Advanced Spanish

FEMA Incident Command

Instructors Glock Course

Precision Immobilization Techniques

Radiation Detection Course

Appendix II

Fatal Errors – You can never be reminded of these too often.

1. **Attitude** - The failure to keep your mind on the job. Remember the section on attention.

2. **Tombstone Courage** - Your failure to action when you should wait for back up.

3. **Rest** – This one topic is considered by most research today to be one of the most important of the errors. There is no replacement for the necessary hours of sleep on your performance.

4. **Bad Positioning** – You have to be aware of every situation you encounter in order to position yourself safely with the tactics we discuss.

5. **Recognizing Danger** - You have to have the attention and understanding to see the little events proposed to you each time you come across someone. It is mind numbing to think how often someone has thought about doing harm to you while in the performance of your duties.

6. **Hands** – These are the two primary body parts of the suspects that you will encounter which will cause you harm. Know where they are and what is in them at every second of your encounter.

7. **Relaxing Too Soon** – Another word for this is complacency. Never trust the person you have encountered.

8. **Handcuffing** – This is usually the lack of handcuffing or poor handcuffing tactics. You can always take them off later, but if you are suspicious enough to detain them, handcuff them. It eliminates the threat of number 6.

9. **Search** – When the conditions are correct and safe, conduct a search. If there is a need to search and not just a quick pat down, remember number 8.

10. **Equipment** – Know your equipment, be proficient with your equipment, and understand the need for back up equipment for your primary tools.

Appendix III

Fatal Law Enforcement Flaws

1. Failure to wait for back up.

2. The failure to draw your weapon when the situation called for it.

3. Tunnel vision when dealing with more than one suspect.

4. Failure to keep people in their cars.

5. Proper vehicle placement after a traffic stop.

6. Failure to immediately control a known suspect.

7. Mental planning of different scenarios.

ABOUT THE AUTHOR

Trooper Steven Varnell is a law enforcement training specialist recently retired after serving over 29 years with the Florida Highway Patrol. During his career he worked Patrol, Field Training, Criminal Interdiction, SRT, and K9. He has instructed Firearms, Baton, Felony Stops, and Criminal Interdiction Courses. He was an adjunct instructor for the Multijurisdictional Counterdrug Task Force Training (MCTFT) Program at St. Petersburg College where he taught Highway Interdiction, Officer Safety, Patrol, and Interviews and Interrogations Classes for law enforcement agencies throughout the country. He was a part of FHP's criminal interdiction pilot program which began in 1983, where he served in interdiction and K9 duties for 27 years. He is one of the most experienced interdiction officers in the country.

Steven Varnell is the author of *Criminal Interdiction*, his first and widely acclaimed book, available through bookstores everywhere. He is a sought out instructor and speaker in the officer safety field. Steve can be reached at criminalinterdiction@live.com and for additional information, go to his website at criminalinterdiction.yolasite.com.